SALTER AIR FRYER COOKBOOK FOR BEGINNERS 2024

1500 Days Frugal, Healthy & Delicious Recipes From Favorite Air Frying Home Cook

Copyright©2023 Corey Potter
All rights reserved. No part of this book may be reproduced
or used in any manner without the prior written permission
of the copyright owner, except for the use of brief quotations
in a book review.
Printed by Amazon in the USA.

Disclaimer : Although the author and publisher have made every effort to ensure that the information in this book was correct at press time, the author and publisher do not assume and hereby disclaim any liability to any party for any loss, damage, or disruption caused by errors or omissions, whether such errors or omissions result from negligence, accident, or any other cause. this book is not intended as a substitute for the medical advice of physicians.

TABLE OF CONTENTS

INTRODUCTION 6

BEEF, PORK & LAMB RECIPES 12

Air Fryer Chuck Roast 12
Air Fryer Bacon Wrapped Serranos 12
Air Fryer Bacon Wrapped Brussel Sprouts 12
Air Fryer Taco Casserole 13
Air Fryer Brown Sugar And Honey Glazed Ham 13
Air Fryer Gingery Pork Meatballs 14
Air Fryer Crispy Chilli Beef Recipe 14
Air Fryer Frozen Meatballs 15
Air Fryer Grilled Ham And Cheese 16
Air Fryer Corn Ribs 16
Air Fryer Beef Empanadas 17

Air Fryer Brown Sugar Pork Chops 17
Air Fryer Country Style Ribs 17
Air Fryer Steak Bites 18
Air Fryer Candied Bacon 18
Air Fryer Armadillo Eggs 19
Air Fryer Cheese Stuffed Meatballs 19
Air Fryer Ham With Pineapple Glaze 20
Air Fryer Pork Tenderloin 21
Air Fryer Easter Pork Roast 21
Air Fryer Bacon Wrapped Brussels Sprouts 22
Air Fryer Prosciutto Wrapped Asparagus 22

SALADS & SIDE DISHES RECIPES 23

Cardamom Roasted Beetroot Salad With Harissa Tahini Sauce 23
Air Fryer Roasted Butternut Squash Salad 23
Air Fryer Pigs In A Blanket 24
Air Fryer Asparagus Salad With Feta Vinaigrette 24
Crispy Parmesan Potato Wedges 25

Air Fryer Roasted Garlic 25
Air Fryer Garlic Knots 25
Artichoke Wings With Vegan Ranch Dip 26
Air Fryer Sweet Potato Casserole 26
Air Fryer Diced Potatoes 27
Air Fryer Kielbasa 28

VEGETABLE & & VEGETARIAN RECIPES 29

Air Fryer Ham And Potato Casserole 29
Air-fryer Green Tomato Stacks 29
Crispy Air Fryer Lemon Broccoli 30
Air Fryer Tofu Bites 30
Roasted Air Fryer Carrots 30
Air Fryer Fried Pickles 31
Hot Cauliflower Wings 31
Easy Air Fryer Radishes 31

Air Fryer Mushrooms 32
Air Fryer Tofu 32
Maple Glazed Roasted Vegetables With Pesto And Spiced Nuts 32
Air Fryer Totchos 33
Air-fried Buffalo Cauliflower 33
Crispy Air Fryer Brussels Sprouts 34
Air Fryer Buffalo Cauliflower 34

Air Fryer Chili Garlic Tofu 34	Air Fryer Roasted Rainbow Carrots 36
Mexican Street Corn 35	Air-fryer Crispy Tofu Recipe 36
Air Fryer Herbed Brussels Sprouts 35	Air Fryer Mushrooms And Onions 36
Air Fryer Twice-baked Potatoes 36	Air Fryer Baked Potato 37

FAVORITE AIR FRYER RECIPES 38

Air Fryer Bagel Pizzas 38	Air Fryer Jalepeno Poppers 43
Air Fryer Taco Calzones 38	Air Fryer Fried Rice 43
Air Fryer Hot Dogs 39	Air Fryer Pizza 43
Air Fryer Frozen Corn Dogs 39	Air Fryer Bratwurst 44
Air Fryer Tostones 39	Air Fryer Nuts And Bolts 44
Air Fried Spicy Duck Leg 39	Classic Margherita Pizza 45
Air Fryer Sausage Rolls 40	Air Fryer Hot Pockets 45
Air Fryer Spaghetti Squash 40	Air Fryer Totino's Pizza 46
Air Fryer Elote 41	Air Fryer Sausages 46
Air Fryer Reheating Leftover Pizza 41	3 Cheese Air Fryer Mini Pizzas 46
Air Fryer Corn Dogs 42	Air Fryer Brats 46
Air Fryer French Bread Pizzas 42	

SNACKS & APPETIZERS RECIPES 47

Air Fryer Potato Chips 47	Curly Fries In The Air Fryer 51
Air-fryer Healthier Veggie Chips 47	Frozen Waffle Fries In The Air Fryer 51
Air Fryer Chickpeas Recipe 47	Air Fryer Baked Sweet Potato 52
Air Fryer Ravioli 48	Air-fryer Pineapple Chips 52
Air Fryer Beet Chips 48	Air Fryer French Fries 52
Air Fryer Frozen Tater Tots 49	Air Fryer Zucchini Chips 52
Air Fryer Potato Skins 49	Air Fryer Curly Fries 53
Air Fryer Puffed Butter Beans 49	Air Fryer Home Fries 53
Crispy Air Fryer Potato Chips 50	Blistered Snap Peas 53
Air Fryer Kale Chips 50	Roasted Garlic Green Beans 54
Avocado Fries With Lime Dipping Sauce 50	Air Fryer Spicy Onion Rings 54
Air Fryer Tortilla Chips 51	

SANDWICHES & BURGERS RECIPES 56

Keto Friendly Game Day Burgers 56	Air Fryer Hamburgers 56

Air Fried Crispy Chicken Sandwiches 56
Air Fryer Grilled Cheese Sandwich 57
Air Fryer Bacon, Egg And Cheese Biscuit Breakfast Sandwiches 57
Air Fryer Frozen Burger 58
Air Fryer Chicken Burgers 58
Greek Lamb Burgers With Baked Eggplant Fries 59
Air Fryer Biscuit Egg Sandwiches 59
Air Fryer Burgers From Frozen Patties 60

FISH & SEAFOOD RECIPES 61

Air Fryer Oven Cheesy Scalloped Potatoes 61
Air Fryer Shrimp 61
Air Fryer Scallops 62
Air Fryer Salmon And Swiss Chard 62
Air Fryer Keto Coconut Shrimp 62
Air Fryer Bacon Wrapped Scallops 63
Air Fryer Blackened Mahi Mahi 63
Fish 'n' Chips 64
Air-fried Beer Battered Fish Tacos With Mango Salsa Recipe 64
Frozen Shrimp In The Air Fryer 65
Air Fryer Salmon With Maple Soy Glaze 65
Air Fryer Crispy Fish Fillets 65
Cajun Air Fryer Fish 66
Air Fryer Salmon In 6 Minutes Tender And Flaky 66
Air Fryer Bacon Wrapped Shrimp 67
Air-fryer Fish Tacos 67
Air Fryer Tilapia 68
Air Fryer Fish Tacos 68
Air Fryer Shrimp Fajitas 69
Air Fryer Fried Shrimp 69
Air Fryer Mahi Mahi 70
Air Fryer Breaded Shrimp 70
Crisp-skinned Air Fryer Salmon With Salsa Verde 71

POULTRY RECIPES 72

Dry Rubbed Wings With A Gorgonzola Dipping Sauce 72
Air Fryer Tandoori Turkey Breast 72
Air Fryer Whole Chicken 73
Air-fryer Crispy Salt And Pepper Chicken Wings Recipe 73
Air Fryer Chicken Katsu 74
Air Fryer Whole Turkey With Gravy 74
Air Fryer Doritos Crusted Chicken Strips 75
Air Fryer Chicken Drumsticks 75
Cauliflower Rice Arancini 76
Air Fryer Chicken Parmesan Recipe 76
Air Fryer Chicken, Broccoli, And Onions 77
Butter Chicken 78
Air Fryer Nashville Hot Chicken Hack 79
General Tso's Air-fryer Chicken 80
Air Fryer Chili Crisp Crunch Chicken Wings 80
Air Fryer Lebanese Chicken 81
Air Fryer 'kfc' Fried Chicken 82
Air Fryer Chicken Bites With Parmesan Cheese 82
Air Fryer Chicken Thighs With Salsa Verde And Lemony Kale Salad 83
Crispy Sesame Chicken 84
Air Fryer Chicken Nuggets 84
Broccoli And Cheese Stuffed Chicken 85
Air Fryer Buffalo Chicken Livers With Blue Cheese Dipping Sauce 86

DESSERTS RECIPES 87

- Homemade Strawberry Twists 87
- Zucchini Chocolate Chip Cookies 87
- Air Fried Marshmallow Peeps 88
- Diet Friendly Avocado Brownies 88
- Shrunken Apple Punch 88
- Roasted Pears & Shortbread 89
- Air Fryer Fried Peach Pie 89
- Air Fryer Donuts 90
- Air Fryer Apple Chips 91
- St Patrick's Day Air Fryer Oven Chocolate Guinness Cupcakes 91
- Apple Cider Snickerdoodles 92
- Strawberry Pretzel Pie 92
- Easy Air Fryer Donuts 93
- Red Velvet Cake Parfaits 93
- Air-fryer Hot-cross-bun Ice-cream Balls 94
- Air Fryer Blueberry Scones 94
- Caramelized Banana Pudding Cups 94
- Air Fryer Mint Aero Danish 95
- Frozen Grands Biscuits In Air Fryer 95
- Air-fryer Apple Fritters 96
- Air Fryer Oatmeal Cookies 96
- Basque Burnt Cheesecake 97
- Baked Apple Cider Donuts 97

BREAKFAST & BRUNCH RECIPES 99

- Air Fryer Cinnamon Roll Bites 99
- Air Fryer Lasagna Egg Rolls 99
- Air Fryer "pretzel" Bites & Irish Pub Beer Cheese ... 100
- Air Fryer French Toast Sticks 100
- Air Fryer French Onion Corn On The Cob 101
- Air Fryer Croutons 101
- Frozen Egg Rolls In The Air Fryer 101
- Air Fryer Spinach, Roasted Red Pepper, And Goat Cheese Omelet 102
- Air Fryer Hard Boiled Eggs 102
- Air Fryer Blueberry Baked Oats 102
- Crispy Spinach Tacos 103
- Air Fryer Crispy Breaded Cauliflower Bites 103
- Air Fryer Breakfast Burritos 104
- Air Fryer Eggplant Parmesan 104
- Air Fryer Mini Egg, Ham, And Cheese Quiche 105
- Air Fryer Soft Boiled Eggs 105
- Air Fryer Brisket Tacos 105
- Air Fryer Zucchini Pizza Bites 106
- Air Fryer Hash Brown Egg Bites 106
- Air Fryer Baked Oats 107
- Air Fryer Pasta Tacos 107
- Air Fryer Avocado Eggs 108
- Air Fryer Frozen Hash Brown Patties 108

INTRODUCTION

An air fryer is a kitchen appliance that allows you to cook foods with hot air instead of oil. It's like having your mini convection oven on your countertop! Air fryers rapidly circulate hot air around the food inside the basket or tray. This creates a crispy exterior while locking in moisture and flavor inside. Unlike deep frying or baking in oil, there's no need for excess oils or fats when using an air fryer, making it a healthier cooking option overall. Using my air fryer has become second nature now that I understand its functionality. With adjustable temperature controls and various settings, including pre-programmed modes for specific foods like chicken wings or French fries – cooking with my air fryer feels effortless and foolproof. Plus, it cooks frozen foods well, and fresh veggies are given a new life thanks to this nifty appliance!

BENEFITS OF USING AN AIR FRYER FOR COOKING CANNED FOODS

HEALTHIER COOKING METHOD

I love using my air fryer for cooking canned foods because it's healthier than deep-frying. Using hot air instead of oil makes the food crispy without adding unnecessary calories and fat. This technique also helps retain more nutrients, making it an excellent option for those who want to eat healthily. I don't have to worry about that greasy feeling after eating fried foods. Air frying canned vegetables like green beans or baked goods like biscuits can be a tasty way to enjoy them without all the added fats from traditional frying methods. For example, when I air fry canned green beans with some seasoning and a touch of oil spray, they come out perfectly crispy on the outside and tender on the inside – just what I'm looking for in a side dish! It's amazing how such simple changes can make our meals healthier while tasting delicious. Overall, using an air fryer as an alternative cooking method is perfect for those who want to cut back on oily or fatty foods but still enjoy satisfying snacks and meals. Learning how to cook canned foods in my air fryer has been fun and rewarding as someone who loves experimenting with different recipes and ingredients.

TIME-SAVING

Using an air fryer to cook canned foods is not only healthier but also a time-saving method.
You can have your favorite canned foods cooked in just minutes with the right temperature and timing settings. Compared to traditional cooking methods such as baking or frying, an air fryer reduces cooking time by about 20-30%. It saves cooking time, and cleanup is faster and easier with an air fryer. Unlike conventional ovens or stovetops that require multiple pots and pans, air fryers typically have one removable basket that's easy to clean. Plus, they don't produce much smoke or odor during cooking, making them ideal for quick meals on busy days.

VERSATILITY IN COOKING DIFFERENT TYPES OF CANNED FOODS

One of the most significant benefits of air frying canned foods is its versatility in cooking different canned foods. You can cook almost anything in a can using an air fryer, from vegetables and meats to baked goods, seafood, snacks, and appetizers. For example, canned green beans are a popular vegetable easily cooked in an air fryer for a healthier alternative to traditional fried green beans. And if you're looking for something more substantial, try making honey-barbecue chicken wings or spicy tuna cakes using your air fryer. The possibilities are endless when it comes to cooking canned foods in an air fryer. With so many options available, knowing which canned foods work best for air frying and how to prepare them properly before placing them inside the appliance is essential.

With these tips and tricks under your belt, you'll be on your way to creating delicious meals with ease!

REDUCED OIL USAGE
One of the most significant benefits of cooking canned foods in an air fryer is the reduced use of oil. Unlike traditional frying methods, you only need a fraction of the oil to achieve crispy and delicious results. This makes it a healthier alternative for those conscious of their calorie intake. With less oil usage, air frying also minimizes the risk of ingesting harmful substances in heated oils. Compared to deep-frying or sautéing, air frying allows you to cook your favorite canned foods with minimal added fats without compromising taste and texture. By choosing the suitable types of canned foods and coating them lightly with seasoning or batter, you'll have a guilt-free pleasure that will satisfy your cravings without sacrificing your health goals.

CHOOSING THE BEST CANNED FOODS FOR AIR FRYING
When choosing canned foods to air fry, consider the types of vegetables, meats, baked goods, seafood, and snacks that can be fried with reduced oil usage and increased crispiness.

VEGETABLES---I love air frying vegetables because they are healthier and deliver crispy and delicious results. My favorite canned vegetables to cook in the air fryer are green beans and corn, but you can use almost any vegetable you have on hand. Just remember to drain excess liquid before coating them with seasoning or batter. One crucial tip for air frying veggies is not to overcrowd the basket. This ensures that each piece gets evenly cooked and crispy. I also recommend setting the temperature between 375-400°F and cooking for 8-12 minutes, depending on your desired level of crispiness. And if you want an added flavor, try tossing your veggies in a bit of melted butter or oil mixed with herbs or spices before adding them to the basket!

MEATS---Meats can be a delicious addition to your air fryer repertoire. Some great canned meat options include chicken, beef, and pork. Before cooking, drain any excess liquid from the can and pat dry with paper towels. When preparing canned meats for air frying, you can coat them in various seasonings or batter for added flavor and texture. Remember that wet batter should be avoided as it will not cook evenly in the air fryer. Instead, use a dry coating or spices like paprika or garlic powder. By following these tips and experimenting with different recipes, you'll soon discover how versatile your air fryer can be when cooking canned meats!

BAKED GOODS---Baked goods are a delicious addition to any meal and can be made even better using an air fryer. Canned biscuits, cinnamon rolls, and gingerbread bites are just a few examples of baked goods that can be made in the air fryer. The reduced oil usage makes them healthier and creates a crispy outer layer. When preparing canned baked goods for air frying, it's important to coat them with seasoning or batter before cooking. This will help enhance their flavor and create an even crispier texture. Wet batter foods should not be placed in the air fryer since they tend to cook unevenly, while corn dogs should be pre-fried before being air fried for best results. Following these tips and tricks, you can enjoy perfectly cooked canned baked goods straight from your trusty air fryer!

SEAFOOD---I love cooking seafood in my air fryer. It's a healthier alternative to deep frying and cooks the fish to a perfect crisp. My favorite canned seafood to air fry include shrimp, crab cakes, and even tuna patties. Before you air fry your seafood, drain any excess liquid from the can and season it with your preferred spices or batter for extra flavor. Set your air fryer temperature between 350-400 degrees Fahrenheit, depending on the type of fish you're cooking, and cook them for about 5-8 minutes per side until they are crispy on the outside and tender on the inside. Remember not to overcrowd your air fryer basket, which can cause uneven cooking or lead to food sticking together. With these simple tips, you'll be able to enjoy perfectly cooked canned seafood every time!

SNACKS AND APPETIZERS---Don't forget about snacks and appetizers when it comes to air-frying canned foods. Air fryers can create deliciously crispy and healthier versions of favorite crunchy snacks like popcorn or kale chips. For a heartier snack or party appetizer, try air-frying frozen meatballs or chicken wings for a quick cook time and crispy texture. Remember that wet batter foods should be avoided in the air fryer, but a light coating of seasoning or breadcrumbs can add extra flavor to your snack creations. Another great option for snacking is air-fried sweet potato fries. Sweet potatoes are an excellent source of vitamins A and C and are perfect for those seeking a healthier alternative to traditional french fries. Slice the sweet potatoes into thin strips, coat them with oil and seasoning, then pop them into the air fryer until crispy and tender. With these tasty options, your next game-day spread will be a hit!

PREPARING CANNED FOODS FOR AIR FRYING

Before air frying canned foods, it's essential to drain excess liquid from them and coat them with seasoning or batter for added flavor and texture.

Draining Excess Liquid

When preparing canned foods for air frying, one essential step is draining excess liquid. This is because too much liquid can cause steam, making your food come out soggy instead of crispy. Ensure you use a strainer or colander to drain any excess water while shaking it well to prevent dripping. For best results, it's recommended that you pat dry the canned foods with paper towels after draining off any liquids. Doing this helps remove more moisture from the food and provides a dry surface for seasoning or coating with batter. By draining excess liquid before cooking, your air-fried canned foods will come out deliciously crispy and perfectly cooked inside!

Coating With Seasoning Or Batter

When it comes to air frying canned foods, adding seasoning or batter can make a world of difference in taste and texture. Try coating vegetables like green beans or sliced potatoes with breadcrumbs mixed with your favorite spices for crispy results. Mix cinnamon and sugar and dredge slices of canned pineapple before placing them in the air fryer for a sweeter option. However, it's important to note that wet batter should not be used when cooking canned foods in an air fryer. The high heat from the appliance will cause the batter to blow around inside the basket and cook unevenly. Instead, opt for dry coatings like panko breadcrumbs or crushed cornflakes for that perfect crunch without making a mess.

Setting Up Your Air Fryer For Cooking Canned Foods

To ensure your canned foods are cooked to perfection in your air fryer, it's vital to set up the appliance correctly – this includes selecting the right temperature and time settings and preheating the basket. Read on for more tips and tricks on making the most out of your air fryer when cooking canned foods!

Temperature And Time Settings
When it comes to air frying canned foods, setting the right temperature and time is crucial for a successful outcome. It's always best to refer to the manual that came with your air fryer for guidance. Generally, most air fryers have a temperature range between 200-400°F, and cooking times can vary between 5-25 minutes depending on your cooking. Preheating your air fryer beforehand is also essential, ensuring even cooking and better results. Once preheated, adjust the temperature settings and watch the food cook. It's always helpful to shake or flip your food halfway through cooking time for an evenly cooked result. Remember, every dish has unique temperature requirements, so consult recipe instructions before starting.

Preheating The Air Fryer
Preheating your air fryer ensures that your canned foods cook evenly and crisp. To preheat your air fryer, set the temperature to the recommended level and allow it to heat up for a few minutes before adding your food. It's important not to overcrowd the basket during this process as it can affect the cooking time. Once preheated, place your canned foods in the basket and set the timer according to the recipe or instructions on the packaging. Remember to check on your food halfway through cooking, using tongs or a spatula to flip them over for even cooking. By taking these steps and following our helpful tips, you'll be able to achieve deliciously crispy canned foods cooked in an air fryer every time!

CLEANING YOUR AIR FRYER PROPERLY
Cleaning your air fryer properly is crucial to maintaining its efficiency and prolonging lifespan. This includes removing excess grease and food debris, wiping down the interior and exterior of the appliance, as well as checking and replacing the air filter regularly.

Removing excess grease and food debris
I always make sure to clean my air fryer properly after each use. To remove excess grease and food debris, I use a damp cloth or sponge to wipe down the exterior and interior of the appliance. It's important to be gentle while cleaning to not damage the non-stick coating. Another helpful tip is removing leftover crumbs or debris from the bottom of the basket using a kitchen brush or toothbrush. Add dish soap and water to your cloth or sponge for extra cleaning power if there are stubborn stains. Keeping your air fryer clean and free from buildup will perform better and last longer overall.

Wiping Down the Interior And Exterior Of The Air Fryer
Keeping your air fryer clean is essential to prevent buildup and ensure optimal performance. Wiping down the interior and exterior of the air fryer is crucial in maintaining its longevity. After each use, allow the appliance to cool before unplugging it and wiping down the inside with a damp cloth. To clean the exterior of your air fryer, wipe it down with a damp cloth or sponge. Avoid using harsh chemicals or abrasive materials that could damage the surface. Regular cleaning will keep your appliance looking new and prevent any unwanted odors from forming while cooking different types of foods. Remember to also check and replace your air filter regularly per manufacturer instructions. This ensures that airflow remains consistent during cooking, resulting in evenly cooked food every time you prepare something delicious in your beloved air fryer!

Checking And Replacing The Air Filter Regularly
A critical aspect of maintaining your air fryer is regularly checking and replacing the air filter. The air filter ensures that your appliance operates properly by preventing dust and other particles from entering the heating element. Over time, the air filter can become dirty, clogged, or damaged, affecting its ability to trap debris effectively. To check the condition of your air filter, gently remove it from its slot at the back of the unit. If you notice any signs of damage or excessive buildup on the filter, it's time to replace it with a new one. Most manufacturers recommend replacing your air filter every three months for optimal performance and longevity of your appliance. By checking and replacing your air filters regularly, you'll enjoy better-tasting foods cooked in a cleaner environment while extending the lifespan of your valuable kitchen gadget.

AIR FRYERS FREQUENTLY ASKED QUESTIONS
Can I put oil in an air fryer? ----- Most recipes only call for about 1 tablespoon of oil, which is best applied with a mister. Fatty foods, like bacon, won't need you to add any oil. Leaner meats, however, will need some oiling to keep them from sticking to the pan.

What shouldn't you put in an Air Fryer? ----- The Air Fryer is one of those kitchen inventions that seem too good to be true. You can cook practically any food in the hot air multi-cooker. However, there are mistakes a lot of us do when handling an air fryer including not preheating your air fryer, not giving the air fryer enough space, overcrowding the air fryer basket, using too little oil, cutting vegetables too small, using wet batters and not washing the air fryer often enough.

Can I use Aluminum Foil or Baking Paper in the Air Fryer? ----- As a general rule, you can use both on the bottom of the air fryer if the basket sits on top. Using aluminum foil or baking paper in the basket technically can be done as long as it's weighed down by the food however it's not recommended because an air fryer works by providing a constant air flow around the cooking cavity.

Should I shake the basket while cooking? ----- Yes, shaking is allowed. A number of foods will stick to the basket if you don't shake it while cooking. Giving it a little shake is specially helpful if you overlap foods, this way the contents of the basket will cook evenly.

What's the first thing I should cook in my new Air Fryer? ----- The most common foods to start with are French Fries, and also Chicken Drumsticks.

What are the disadvantages to cooking in an Air Fryer? ----- The only real disadvantage to cooking in an air fryer is the fact most of the air fryers on the market have small cooking cavities.

What kind of foods can you cook in an Air Fryer? ----- The air fryer is your ticket to healthier fried foods that still taste crispy-crunchy delicious and leaves you with a lot less mess at clean-up time. Whether frozen food or raw meat or reheating leftover food, the hot air multi-cooker does a fantastic job. Having an air fryer means you can go ahead and cook frozen food such as frozen fries, nuggets, fish sticks etc. You can also cook raw meat, for example you can roast chicken or pork in the fryer. And you can certainly roast vegetables and nuts too and let's not forget you can easily bake small items.

Should I pause the Air Fryer when checking on the food? ----- Since you generally only spend a matter of seconds checking, or shaking the food, it is not necessary to pause the air fryer.

Can I open the Air Fryer while cooking? ----- Every Air Fryer is slightly different however going on the premise that heat rises, if your air fryer opens by sliding a basket out from the side or front, then there should be no reason why you can't open the basket for short periods of time.

Should I preheat the Air Fryer? ----- Every Air Fryer manufacturer will have their own recommendations for their particular air fryer. This is also a good idea since many users find that cooking times are more accurate if you preheat first.

Why are my cooking times different? -----Remember, not all Air Fryers are created equal. Air Fryers work by circulating hot air around the food. The internal shape of the Air Fryer and how the air flows, as well as how hot the air is all contribute to how long it takes to cook a food. This is why you should check often and only use temperatures as a guide until you know how your particular Air Fryer cooks.

What are the advantages to cooking in an Air Fryer? ----- Advantages are many, like we said before, we're talking about a healthier form of cooking. Even though your food is fried it won't be dripping with oil. It's less expensive to run. Cooking in an air fryer is very quick. Also, food cooked in an air fryer is generally really tasty simply because the food is crispy on the outside, and juicy and tender on the inside.

BEEF, PORK & LAMB RECIPES

Air Fryer Chuck Roast

Servings: 6
Cooking Time: 45 Minutes

Ingredients:
- 2 pounds beef chuck roast
- 1 tablespoon olive oil
- ½ tablespoon Worcestershire sauce
- 1 ½ teaspoons kosher salt
- 1 ½ teaspoons garlic powder
- 1 teaspoon onion powder
- 1 teaspoon dried thyme
- 1 teaspoon dried rosemary
- 1 teaspoon black pepper

Directions:
1. Line the inside of your air fryer with aluminum foil. Preheat the air fryer to 390 degrees F.
2. In a small bowl, whisk together olive oil and Worcestershire sauce. In a second small bowl, combine the salt, garlic powder, onion powder, thyme, rosemary, and pepper.
3. Rub the roast with the olive oil-Worcestershire sauce mixture, then rub the herb mixture over the entire roast. Place the roast in the basket of your air fryer.
4. Air fry for 15 minutes, then carefully flip the roast. Air fry at 320 degrees F for another 45-60 minutes, depending on the size of the roast.
5. Remove, allow to rest for 10 minutes, then slice and serve with your favorite sides.

Air Fryer Bacon Wrapped Serranos

Ingredients:
- 12 Serrano peppers
- 12 Slices partially Cooked bacon
- 2 String Mozarella Cheeses

Directions:
1. Partially cook the bacon in the air fryer at 300° for 3 minutes on each side. Place onto paper towel and set aside.
2. Cut the tops off the serrano peppers and carefully slice down one side of the pepper(do not cut all the way through). Fold open the pepper and remove seeds.
3. Peel pieces of the string cheese and stuff the peppers. Wrap the bacon around each pepper tightly then place into air fryer basket.
4. Air fry at 350° for 5 minutes or until desired bacon crispiness.

Air Fryer Bacon Wrapped Brussel Sprouts

Servings: 4
Cooking Time: 13 Minutes

Ingredients:
- 8 slices bacon regular and sliced in half
- 16 small Brussels sprouts
- ¼ cup brown sugar

Directions:
1. Wrap one slice of halved bacon around each brussels sprout, seal with a toothpick if necessary. Repeat until all sprouts have been wrapped.
2. In a large glass bowl, toss wrapped sprouts with brown sugar, until they are well coated.
3. Place in the air fryer basket, without stacking or overlapping.
4. Air Fry at 380 degrees F for 13-16 minutes, until bacon is crispy.

Notes
Variations
Change up the flavor of bacon - You can use salty bacon, crispy bacon, thick cut bacon, or any piece of bacon or strip of bacon that you want. Maple bacon sounds like some pretty good strips of bacon to add to this easy recipe!

Add toppings - Let's be truthful here and say that toppings are always a crowd-pleaser. Drizzling some olive oil with salt and black pepper on top of this delicious appetizer adds taste in an easy way.

You can add soy sauce to these tender brussels sprouts after they are done cooking, or add some sweetness with a drizzle of maple syrup!

Air Fryer Taco Casserole

Servings: 4
Cooking Time: 20 Minutes

Ingredients:
- 1 lb lean ground beef 95% lean
- 3 tbsp taco seasoning
- 1/4 cup water
- 1/2 cup bell pepper chopped
- 10 oz diced tomatoes and green chilis not drained
- 4 large eggs
- 1/4 cup sour cream
- 1/3 cup heavy cream
- 1/2 cup cheddar cheese shredded
- 1 tbsp green onions optional

Directions:
1. Brown the lean ground beef in a skillet over medium heat, about 5 minutes or until no longer pink. Drain.
2. Add the water, taco seasoning, diced bell pepper, and canned tomatoes with green chilis. Stir and simmer for 3 minutes.
3. Preheat the Air Fryer to 300 degrees Fahrenheit. Prepare the air fryer casserole/cake dish.
4. In a medium mixing bowl, whisk the eggs, sour cream, and heavy cream together. Set aside.
5. Pour the taco meat mixture into the bottom of the prepared casserole pan. Top the meat mixture with the egg mixture.
6. Place the casserole into the air fryer basket and cook for 18 minutes. Top with cheese and cook an additional 2 minutes, or until the cheese is fully melted.
7. Top with green onions and serve.

Notes
Store in an airtight container in the refrigerator for up to 3 days.
Consider adding additional flavors like diced jalapenos for extra spice.
Mix up the flavors by adding a little mozzarella and cream cheese to the dish.
KETO: C/7 P/36 F/25

Air Fryer Brown Sugar And Honey Glazed Ham

Servings: 10
Cooking Time: 55 Minutes

Ingredients:
- 2-3 pounds (.9-1.36 kg) boneless, fully cooked ham
- BROWN SUGAR GLAZE
- 1/2 cup (110 g) brown sugar
- 1/4 cup (60 ml) honey
- 1/4 cup (60 ml) orange juice (or 1 orange juiced)
- 2 Tablespoons (60 ml) mustard (optional) or apple cider vinegar
- 1/4 teaspoon (1.25 ml) Cinnamon
- 1/4 teaspoon (1.25 ml) Clove
- black pepper , to taste
- Aluminum Foil
- 8" square Baking Pan

Directions:
1. Remove the ham from the fridge and allow to come up to room temperature, about 2 hours before cooking.
2. Make the Glaze: In a small saucepan or microwave safe bowl, combine the brown sugar & honey glaze ingredients (brown sugar, honey, orange juice, optional mustard or apple cider vinegar, cinnamon, clove, and black pepper). Heat (can be done on the stovetop or in the microwave) and whisk until brown sugar is dissolved and glaze is well combined. Set aside.
3. If the ham has a netting, remove it from the ham. If ham is not pre-sliced, score the ham with shallow 1/2-inch criss-cross cuts.

4. For Basket Style Air Fryers: Line the air fryer basket with 2 pieces of long, overlapping foil sheets (see step-by step photos on website write up above). Lay the ham on top of the foil and then brush with some of the glaze to coat the ham. Close the foil over the ham and wrap tightly.
5. For Oven Style Air Fryers: Place the ham in an 8"x8" baking pan which fits in your air fryer (you may need to trim the edges of the ham to fit your pan and air fryer size). Brush with some of the glaze and close foil over the ham, wrapping tightly.
6. Air Fry at 340°F/170°C for 25 minutes. Open the foil and brush the ham with more glaze (make sure to reserve some glaze for finishing & serving). Close the foil tightly, and Air Fry again at 340°/170°C for 25 minutes.
7. After air frying for the 50 minutes, open up the foil again and now push the foil down around the edges of the ham if using the basket-style air fryer method. Create a boat with the foil that holds the juices and keeps the ham from drying out. If using the Oven Style Air Fryer method, just remove the foil from the 8"x8" pan.
8. Brush with a little more glaze and increase heat to Air Fry at 360°F/180°C for about 5 minutes, or until caramelized to your liking.
9. Let ham rest for 5 minutes before serving.
10. Optional serving: Combine the juices from the air fryer basket and the remaining glaze in a saucepan. Bring to a simmer and cook for about 5 minutes or until thickened. Brush the glaze onto the ham when serving or serve in a bowl.

Air Fryer Gingery Pork Meatballs

Servings: 4

Ingredients:
- FOR NOODLES
- 6 oz. rice noodles
- 1/2 c. Asian-style sesame dressing
- 1 large carrot, shaved with julienne peeler or cut into matchsticks
- 1/2 English cucumber, shaved with julienne peeler or cut into matchsticks
- 1 scallion, thinly sliced
- 1/4 c. cilantro, chopped
- FOR MEATBALLS
- 1 large egg
- 2 tsp. grated lime zest plus 2 Tbsp lime juice
- 1 1/2 tbsp. honey
- 1 tsp. fish sauce
- Kosher salt
- 1/2 c. panko
- 1 cloves garlic, grated
- 2 scallions, finely chopped
- 1 tbsp. grated fresh ginger
- 1 small jalape?o, seeds removed, finely chopped
- 1 lb. ground pork
- 1/4 c. cilantro, chopped

Directions:
1. Prepare noodles: Cook noodles per package directions. Rinse under cold water to cool, drain well and transfer to large bowl. Toss with dressing, carrot, cucumber and scallion; set aside.
2. Prepare meatballs: In large bowl, whisk together egg, lime zest and lime juice, honey, fish sauce and ? teaspoon salt; stir in panko and let sit 1 minute. Stir in garlic, scallions, ginger and jalape?o, then add pork and cilantro and mix to combine.
3. Shape into Tbsp-size balls and air-fry at 400F (in batches, if necessary; balls can touch but should not be stacked), shaking basket occasionally, until browned and cooked through, 8 to 12 minutes. Fold cilantro into noodles and serve with meatballs.

Air Fryer Crispy Chilli Beef Recipe

Ingredients:
- For the crispy beef
- 450g Beef Strips
- 4 tbsp Cornflour
- 2 tsp Sesame Oil
- 1 tsp Chinese 5 Spice
- 1 tsp Chilli Powder

- ½ tsp Salt
- ½ tsp Black Pepper
- For the sauce
- 200ml Beef Stock
- 4 tbsp Rice Wine Vinegar
- 2 tbsp Sweet Chilli Sauce
- 2 tbsp Sesame Oil
- 1 tbsp Soy Sauce
- 1 tbsp Tomato Puree
- 1 tbsp Honey
- 1 tsp Ginger
- 2 Cloves Garlic, Crushed
- 2 Spring Onions, Chopped
- 1 Red Chilli, Chopped
- 1 Red Pepper, Sliced
- 1 Green Pepper, Sliced

Directions:

1. Add the cornflour, Chinese 5 spice, black pepper, salt, and chili powder to a bowl and stir together.
2. Add beef strips to the bowl and ensure they are fully coated in cornflour mixture.
3. Drizzle 1 tsp of sesame oil at the bottom of the air fryer and add the beef strips in a single layer. Top with another tsp of sesame oil.
4. Cook the beef strips in the air fryer for 10 minutes at 200°C until crispy.
5. Meanwhile, add together the soy sauce, tomato puree, sweet chili, honey, rice wine vinegar, beef stock, and 1 tbsp of sesame oil and stir thoroughly. Set aside.
6. Heat up 1 tbsp of sesame oil in a frying pan and add the crushed garlic and chopped red chilli and stir together.
7. Add the 2 chopped spring onions, sliced red pepper and sliced green pepper to the pan, then add your mixed together sauce and stir through all the vegetables and cook this on high heat until the sauce has thickened.
8. Finally, add the crispy beef and coat it in the sauce.
9. When everything is coated and cooked, serve with egg noodles or rice and top with fresh chilies, spring onions, and sesame seeds.

Air Fryer Frozen Meatballs

Servings: 3

Cooking Time: 10 Minutes

Ingredients:

- 1 lb. (454 g) Frozen Meatballs (16 oz./454g)
- oil spray , to coat the meatballs
- BBQ or Tomato Sauce , optional
- Oil Sprayer

Directions:

1. Place the frozen meatballs in the air fryer basket and spread out into a single even layer (cook in batches if needed). Coat the meatballs evenly with oil spray.
2. Air Fry at 380°F/195°C for 8-12 minutes (depending on size) or until heated all the way through, gently shaking and turning the meatballs halfway through cooking.
3. If desired, heat your favorite sauce (BBQ, tomato, etc.) & toss or brush the sauce with the meatballs before serving.

Notes

Cook Frozen - Do not thaw first.

Shake or turn as needed. Don't overcrowd the air fryer basket.

Recipe timing is based on a non-preheated air fryer. If cooking in multiple batches back to back, the following batches may cook a little quicker.

Adjust cooking time based off your specific air fryer.

Remember to set a timer to shake/flip/toss as directed in recipe.

Air Fryer Grilled Ham And Cheese

Servings: 4

Cooking Time: 7 Minutes

Ingredients:
- 2 tablespoons mayonnaise
- 8 slices white bread
- 2 tablespoons Dijon mustard
- 8 slices deli ham
- 4 large slices Swiss cheese
- 8 dill pickle slices
- cooking spray

Directions:
1. Spread mayonnaise on one side of each slice of bread. With mayo side down, lightly spread 4 slices of bread with Dijon mustard, evenly top each with Swiss cheese, ham slices, folded to fit, and pickle slices. Place the remaining 4 bread slices on the sandwiches, mayo side up, and lightly press sandwiches to close.
2. Preheat the air fryer to 380 degrees F (193 degrees C). Spray the air fryer basket with cooking spray or line with a parchment liner.
3. Place sandwiches in the air fryer basket in a single layer, leaving some space around them. You may have to cook the sandwiches in batches, depending on the size of your fryer.
4. Cook until sandwiches begin to brown, 3 to 4 minutes. Flip, and cook until cheese has melted and sandwiches are golden brown, 2 to 3 minutes more. Slice sandwiches in half and serve warm.
5. Note:
6. Mayonnaise is the only thing I use these days on grilled sandwiches. It's always ready, spreads easily, browns beautifully, and has no mayo flavor. But you can use butter, if you prefer. Air fryer cooking times may vary depending on the brand and size. So watch your sandwiches closely, especially toward the end of cooking.

Air Fryer Corn Ribs

Servings: 4

Cooking Time: 12 Minutes

Ingredients:
- 2 ears of corn fresh
- 1 Tablespoon butter unsalted
- 1/4 teaspoon garlic powder
- 1/4 teaspoon salt Kosher
- 1/2 teaspoon smoked paprika
- 1/2 teaspoon ground black pepper
- 1/2 teaspoon dried parsley
- fresh parsley for garnish

Directions:
1. Take each whole ear of corn, remove from the husk.
2. Rub cobs to remove the corn silks from in between the corn kernels and cut off the ends.
3. Place corn on the cobs in a microwave safe bowl covered with a damp paper towel and microwave for 2 minutes.
4. Let corn cobs cool for 5 minutes on a chopping board or until they are cool enough to touch.
5. Use a sharp knife and slice into the corn cobs: cut the corn in halves lengthwise, and then cut halves into quarters, to make 4 pieces per cob of corn.
6. In a small bowl, combine butter, garlic powder, salt, paprika, black pepper and dried parsley.
7. Brush the corn ribs with the seasoning mixture, coating entire corn rib well.
8. In a single layer place the seasoned corn ribs into the air fryer basket.
9. Air fry at 400 degrees F for 12 minutes, flipping halfway through the cooking process.
10. Top with fresh parsley before serving.

Notes
Optional Favorite Dipping Sauce: Ranch dressing, sour cream and chives, Carolina style bbq sauce, chipotle mayo or Greek yogurt with red pepper flakes.

Optional Additional Toppings: Lime wedges, fresh cilantro, fresh coriander or minced garlic butter.

Cooking Tips: Use a pastry brush to apply butter mixture to pieces of corn ribs. Cutting the corn into ribs makes it easier to eat especially for the little ones. For crispier corn cook for an additional 1-2 minutes. Optional Additional Seasonings: Chili powder, lime juice, taco seasoning, chili oil, Elote seasoning, onion powder, cayenne pepper, chipotle powder or smoked salt.

Air Fryer Beef Empanadas

Servings: 8
Cooking Time: 16 Minutes

Ingredients:
- 8 Goya empanada discs (in frozen section, thawed)
- 1 cup picadillo
- 1 egg white (whisked)
- 1 teaspoon water

Directions:
1. Spray the air fryer basket generously with olive oil spray to avoid sticking, or line the basket with air fryer parchment paper.
2. Place 2 tablespoons of the picadillo in the center of each disc. Fold in half and use a fork to seal the edges. Repeat with the remaining dough.
3. Whisk the egg whites with water, then brush the tops of the empanadas.
4. Air fry in a single layer, in batches as needed 350F 8 minutes, turning halfway or until golden. Remove from heat and repeat with the remaining empanadas.

Notes
How to Bake Empanadas in the Oven: If you don't have an air fryer, you can also bake them in the oven at 400 degrees on a nonstick baking sheet for about 18 to 20 minutes until golden.
How to Freeze Empanadas: You can flash freeze the uncooked empanadas on a sheet pan. Once frozen, transfer to a freezer-safe container for up to 3 months.
Air Fry From Frozen: Pop the frozen empanadas right into your air fryer and air fry 350F for about 12 minutes, turning halfway until golden and hot.

Air Fryer Brown Sugar Pork Chops

Servings: 4
Cooking Time: 12 Minutes

Ingredients:
- 4 boneless center cut pork chops 1 ½ – 2 inches thick
- 2 tablespoons brown sugar
- 1 tablespoon paprika
- 1 ½ teaspoons salt
- 1 ½ teaspoons fresh ground black pepper
- 1 teaspoon ground mustard
- ½ teaspoon onion powder
- ¼ teaspoon garlic powder
- 2 tablespoons olive oil

Directions:
1. Preheat air fryer to 400°F on bake.
2. Pat pork chops dry with a paper towel.
3. In a small bowl, mix together all the dry ingredients.
4. Coat the pork chops with olive oil and rub in the mixture.
5. Cook pork chops for 12 minutes, flipping pork chops over after 6 minutes.

Notes
Leftover pork chops will keep in an airtight container in the refrigerator for up to 4 days.

Air Fryer Country Style Ribs

Servings: 5
Cooking Time: 20 Minutes

Ingredients:
- 2 lbs ribs country-style
- 1 tsp smoked paprika
- 1 1/2 tsp garlic powder
- 2 tsp ground black pepper
- 5 oz barbecue sauce

Directions:
1. Rinse the ribs and then pat them dry. Add the garlic powder, smoked paprika, and ground black seasoning to a small bowl and set aside.

2. Preheat the air fryer to 380 degrees Fahrenheit. Prepare the basket of the air fryer with nonstick cooking spray.
3. Rub the ribs with a small amount of the seasoning mixture.
4. Place the ribs in a single layer in the basket of the air fryer. Cook at 380 degrees for 20 minutes. Remove the basket and brush barbecue sauce onto the tops and sides of the ribs. Place back into the air fryer and cook for an additional 2 minutes. Check the internal temperature with a meat thermometer to ensure the pork has reached 145 degrees Fahrenheit.
5. Serve with your favorite sides.

Notes

Store leftover country-style ribs in an airtight container in the refrigerator for up to 3 days.

This recipe was made using a Cosori 1700 watt 5.8 qt basket style air fryer. All air fryers can cook differently. It's always best to test a small batch before cooking the entire meal to decide if our air fryer requires more or less time.

Air Fryer Steak Bites

Servings: 4
Cooking Time: 6 Minutes

Ingredients:
- 1 pound sirloin steak or strip loin or ribeye
- 1 tablespoon vegetable oil
- 1 tablespoon soy sauce
- 1 ½ teaspoons Worcestershire sauce
- 2 cloves garlic minced
- 1 tablespoon melted salted butter
- salt & pepper to taste
- 1 tablespoon fresh parsley

Directions:

1. Cut steak into 1-inch cubes. Toss with oil, soy sauce, Worcestershire sauce, garlic, salt & pepper. Marinate 15 minutes.
2. Preheat air fryer to 400°F.
3. Remove the steak bites from the marinade and dab dry. Toss with melted butter.
4. Add steak bites to the air fryer basket in a single layer and cook 6-7 minutes or until browned. Do not overcook.
5. Toss with parsley and additional butter if desired. Serve with horseradish sauce below.

Notes

Cook steak bites in batches if needed. Do not overcrowd the air fryer.

Whisk together the following for Horseradish Dipping Sauce:

¼ cup sour cream

2 tablespoons mayonnaise

1 ½ tablespoons prepared horseradish

1 teaspoon fresh lemon juice

1 small clove garlic

salt & pepper to taste

Air Fryer Candied Bacon

Servings: 4
Cooking Time: 10 Minutes

Ingredients:
- 1 pound bacon
- ¼ cup brown sugar

Directions:

1. Place bacon slices in a shallow dish with brown sugar. Toss bacon slices well so both sides are coated with brown sugar.
2. Place slices in the air fryer basket, working in batches so they don't overlap while air frying.
3. Air fry at 380 degrees F for 10-12 minutes until bacon is crispy. Remove slices and place on a cooling rack or on a plate to cool before eating.

Notes

No matter if you call this millionaire bacon or billionaire bacon, everyone will agree that this pig candy is yummy! I like to use dark brown sugar for this recipe as it makes it a delicious treat.

Cooking the bacon in the air fryer is also a great way to keep the bacon grease separate from the bacon, as it will fall through the bottom of the air fryer basket.

But did you know that you can actually use that leftover bacon grease for other air fryer recipes and cooking recipes? I'll save it and store it in a jar and then use it for cooking at other times. (It's really good to use when you're popping popcorn!)

Air Fryer Armadillo Eggs

Servings: 6
Cooking Time: 15 Minutes

Ingredients:
- 1 pound pork sausage ground
- 1 pound bacon 12 slices
- 6 medium jalapenos
- 4 ounces cream cheese room temperature
- 1/2 cup shredded cheddar cheese
- 1 cup Honey BBQ Sauce

Directions:
1. Rinse the jalapeno peppers and pat dry, then slice in half. Remove stems, membrane, and seeds, then set aside.
2. In a medium bowl, combine the cheddar and cream cheese. Generously spoon the cream cheese mixture into one of the halves of the jalapeno and then place two halves together.
3. Divide the pork sausage into six even portions. Flatten a portion of the sausage and fold around a jalapeno, pinch meat to completely seal and cover jalapeno, while shaping into an oval egg shape. Repeat until all jalapenos are covered with sausage.
4. Wrap each covered jalapeno with two slices of bacon, wrapping each piece of bacon with tight wrap, securing with toothpicks.
5. Place in the air fryer basket and air fry at 380 for 15-17 minutes until sausage reaches an internal temperature of 160 degrees F and bacon is crispy. Use a meat thermometer to confirm doneness.
6. Using a basting brush or spoon, brush egg with barbecue sauce before serving.

Notes
VARIATIONS and TIPS:
You can use flavored bacon like smoky bacon or Hickory bacon.
For higher heat level, and spicy peppers, leave some of the membrane.
There are other types of cheese blend you can add for a creamy cheese mixture. Shredded Monterey jack, mozzarella cheese, pepper jack, or even Mexican blend cheese, will make this a perfect appetizer recipe.
Dip in hot sauce, or for more flavor, try a Korean BBQ sauce or Raspberry Chipotle Sauce.
For a larger crowd, double batch recipe!

Air Fryer Cheese Stuffed Meatballs

Servings: 4
Cooking Time: 7 Minutes

Ingredients:
- 1 pound ground beef
- 1 cup Italian Seasoned Breadcrumbs
- 1/2 cup parmesan cheese grated or shredded
- 1 large egg
- 1 teaspoon garlic minced
- 1/2 teaspoon kosher salt
- 1/4 teaspoon ground black pepper
- 4 pieces string cheese cut into inch in pieces

Directions:
1. In a medium mixing bowl, combine beef, breadcrumbs, parmesan cheese, egg, garlic, salt, and pepper. Stir until meatball mixture is well combined.
2. Use a large spoon or cookie scoop to measure them so they are all the same size (about 2-3 tablespoons of meat).
3. Roll each scoopful into about 2-inch sized meatballs (about the size of a golf ball). Place them on a plate or baking sheet until they are all rolled.
4. Cut string cheese into small pieces, about 1 inch in length. Push a cheese cube into the center of each meatball, and then close them back up around the

piece of cheese, by reshaping the meatball to seal in the cheese.
5. Spray the air fryer basket with cooking spray and place the meatballs in a single layer to the basket.
6. Air fry at 380 degrees F for 7-10 minutes, until the hamburger meat is done. To make sure it's done, use a meat thermometer to read the internal temperature, minimum temperature should be about 160 degrees F.

Notes

Optional Favorite Sauce for Dipping: Because meatballs are so versatile, you can eat them with your favorite marinara sauce, pizza sauce, alfredo sauce, pesto sauce or ranch dressing.

Kitchen Tips: This recipe will make a couple of batches of meatballs. Line basket with parchment paper so meatballs won't stick to the basket and makes for an easier clean up.

Substitutions: If you don't have lean ground beef, you can also use ground turkey, ground lamb, ground chicken, ground pork or a lean ground beef. Mini mozzarella balls are also a great stuffer.

Air Fryer Ham With Pineapple Glaze

Servings: 10
Cooking Time: 1 Hour 20 Minutes

Ingredients:
- 2-3 pounds (907 - 1360 g) boneless, fully cooked ham
- PINEAPPLE JUICE GLAZE
- 1 cup (240 ml) pineapple juice
- 1/2 cup (110 g) brown sugar , or to taste
- 1/2 teaspoon (2.5 ml) ground cinnamon
- 1/4 teaspoon (1.25 ml) ground cloves (optional)
- 1/2 teaspoon (2.5 ml) salt , or to taste
- 3 pineapple rings
- Optional - (a few maraschino cherries or cranberries for garnish)
- Aluminum Foil
- 8" square Baking Pan

Directions:
1. Remove the ham from the fridge and allow to come up to room temperature, about 2 hours before cooking.
2. Make the Glaze: Add pineapple juice, brown sugar, cinnamon, optional ground cloves and salt to pan. Simmer on medium-low heat for about 20 minutes or until is reduced to about half or until it starts to thicken a bit. Remove from heat.
3. If needed, remove the netting from the ham. If ham is not pre-sliced, score the ham with shallow 3/4-inch criss-cross cuts.
4. For Basket Style Air Fryers: Line the air fryer basket with 2 pieces of long, criss-crossed foil sheets. Lay the ham on top of the foil and then brush with some of the glaze to coat the ham. Close the foil over the ham and wrap tightly.
5. For Oven Style Air Fryers: Place the ham in an 8"x8" baking pan which fits in your air fryer (you may need to trim the edges of the ham to fit your pan and air fryer size). Brush with some of the glaze and close foil over the ham, wrapping tightly.
6. Air Fry at 340°F/170°C for 25 minutes. Open the foil and brush the ham with more glaze (make sure to reserve some glaze for finishing & serving).
7. Close the foil tightly, and Air Fry again at 340°/170°C for 25 minutes. After air frying for the 50 minutes, open up the foil again and now push the foil down around the edges of the ham if using the basket-style air fryer method. Create a boat with the foil that holds the juices and keeps the hand from drying out. If using the Oven Style Air Fryer method, just remove the foil from the 8"x8" pan.
8. Add the slices of pineapple on the top of the ham. Spread more glaze over everything.
9. Increase heat to Air Fry at 360°F/180°C for about 5 minutes, or until caramelized to your liking. Let ham rest for 5 minutes before serving. Place the the maraschino cherries or cranberries in the center of the pineapple rings for optional garnish.

10. Optional serving: Combine the juices from the air fryer basket and the remaining glaze in a saucepan. Bring to a simmer and cook for a couple minutes or until slightly thickened. Brush the glaze onto the ham when serving or serve in a bowl.

Air Fryer Pork Tenderloin

Servings: 2
Cooking Time: 22 Minutes

Ingredients:
- 1 pork tenderloin
- 1/2 cup olive oil
- 3 tablespoons soy sauce
- 2 cloves garlic, minced
- 2 tablespoons brown sugar
- 1 tablespoon dijon mustard
- salt and pepper, to taste

Directions:
1. Remove the pork tenderloin from its packaging and place aside.
2. Mix the olive oil, soy sauce, garlic, brown sugar, dijon mustard, and salt and pepper into a bowl then add to a Ziploc gallon bag.
3. Add the pork tenderloin to the bag, close it, and cover it with the marinade. Marinate the pork for 30 minutes, but up to 5 days while refrigerated.
4. Preheat the air fryer to 400 degrees.
5. Remove the pork tenderloin from the bag and place in the air fryer. Cook for 22 to 25 minutes flipping halfway through until it hits 145 degrees internally.
6. Let the air fryer pork tenderloin rest for at least 5 minutes, slice into medallions, and enjoy!

Notes
HOW TO REHEAT PORK TENDERLOIN IN THE AIR FRYER:
Preheat your air fryer to 350 degrees.
Cook pork tenderloin for 3 to 5 minutes, until heated thoroughly and enjoy!
HOW TO COOK FROZEN PORK TENDERLOIN IN THE AIR FRYER:
Place frozen pork tenderloin in the air fryer and turn it to 330 degrees.
Cook the pork tenderloin for 33 to 38 minutes, until it reaches 145 degrees at its thickest point, flipping and basting the marinade above halfway through cooking then enjoy!

Air Fryer Easter Pork Roast

Servings: 4
Cooking Time: 2 Hours 10 Minutes

Ingredients:
- 1 x Pork loin joint
- 1 x Pack of green beans
- 1x Head of broccoli
- 1 x Apple
- 4x Pieces of streaky smoked bacon
- 1x Tinned New Potatoes
- 2x Large Carrots
- 4x Yorkshire Puddings

Directions:
1. Season the pork with salt & pepper. Place pork into drawer 1 of the air fryer at 160 for 1hr 20 mins.
2. Whilst the pork is cooking trim both ends of the green beans, cut the broccoli into florets and peel the carrots and cut into 2cm chunks. Toss all prepared vegetables in a little oil, salt & pepper and set aside.
3. ¼ the apple and cut off the core, wrap with 1 piece of streaky bacon. Pop in the fridge until later on.
4. After 1 hour put the carrots into drawer 2 at 160 and cook for 20 mins.
5. Remove the pork, check it is cooked all the way through and leave to rest on a plate covered loosely with foil.
6. Add the green beans and the broccoli to drawer 2 with the carrots, increase the temp to 200 and cook for 10 mins.
7. Place the potatoes into drawer 1 at 200 and cook for 10 mins.

8. Take the apple pieces out of the fridge and pop them into drawer 1 with the potatoes and cook for a further 10 mins.
9. While plating all the ingredients place the Yorkshires into an empty drawer and cook for 4 mins at 200.
10. Serve with gravy and enjoy! Why not use any leftovers and create delicious pork sandwiches the next day or even try a Leftover Yorkshire Pudding Wrap!

Air Fryer Bacon Wrapped Brussels Sprouts

Servings: 8
Cooking Time: 7 Minutes

Ingredients:
- 1 pound brussels sprouts
- ½ pound bacon
- ⅓ cup maple syrup

Directions:
1. Preheat the air fryer to 375°F.
2. Wash and trim brussels cutting them in half.
3. Cut each piece of bacon into thirds. Wrap bacon around the brussels sprouts.
4. Place seam side down in the air fryer basket and brush with maple syrup.
5. Bake 7-10 minutes or until bacon is crisp and brussels sprouts are tender.

Notes
Brussels sprouts should be cooked in a single layer. If needed, cook in batches.

Air Fryer Prosciutto Wrapped Asparagus

Servings: 4
Cooking Time: 8 Minutes

Ingredients:
- 1 pound asparagus
- 6 ounces prosciutto

Directions:
1. Preheat air fryer to 400°F.
2. Wash and trim the end of the asparagus.
3. Wrap one slice of prosciutto around one asparagus and place in the air fryer basket.
4. Cook for 7-8 minutes or until asparagus is tender and prosciutto is crispy.

SALADS & SIDE DISHES RECIPES

Cardamom Roasted Beetroot Salad With Harissa Tahini Sauce

Servings: 4

Ingredients:
- For the roasted beets
- 500g beetroot (peeled, chopped into 2cm pieces)
- 1 x 400g organic chickpeas (drained, rinsed, patted dry)
- 1 1/2 tbsp olive oil
- 1 tbsp agave nectar
- 2 tsp ground cumin
- 16 Seeds from green cardamom pods (ground in pestle and mortar)
- 1 1/4 tsp sea salt
- 1/2 tsp garlic powder
- 1/4 tsp ground black pepper
- 1 Zest of lemon
- For the sauce
- 80g light tahini
- 190ml lukewarm water
- 1 tbsp rose harissa
- 2 tsp agave nectar
- 1 clove garlic (peeled)
- 1 tsp red wine vinegar
- 1/4 tsp ground cumin
- 1/4 - 1/2 tsp sea salt
- 1/2 - 1 Juice of whole lemon
- For the salad
- 100g pomegranate seeds (roughly 1/2 pomegranate)
- 60g rocket
- 30g walnuts (roughly chopped)
- 20g fresh parsley (roughly chopped)
- 1/2 tsp za'atar
- COOKING MODE
- When entering cooking mode - We will enable your screen to stay 'always on' to avoid any unnecessary interruptions whilst you cook!

Directions:
1. Toss together all of the ingredients for the roasted beets in a large bowl until everything is fully coated.
2. Place the crisper tray into the zone 1 drawer then add the vegetables and insert the drawer back into the unit. Select ROAST, set the temperature to 180°C and the temperature to 25 minutes. Select START/STOP to begin cooking. Shake the drawer every 10 minutes until the cooking time is complete. Remove the drawer and set to one side.
3. Place the ingredients for the sauce into a bullet style blender and blend until smooth. Start with the juice of half a lemon and add more if you feel it needs it. Again if you'd prefer a thinner sauce blend in more water.
4. Toss together the roasted beetroot mixture in a large salad bowl with the remaining salad ingredients then serve immediately with plenty of the sauce drizzled over.

Air Fryer Roasted Butternut Squash Salad

Servings: 4
Cooking Time: 15 Minutes

Ingredients:
- 1 small butternut squash, peeled, seeded, cut into 1-inch pieces
- 4 tablespoons olive oil
- 1 teaspoon 's House Seasoning
- 1/4 teaspoon cayenne pepper
- 2 tablespoons fresh lemon juice
- 1 small shallot, minced
- 1/4 teaspoon salt
- 6 ounces arugula
- 1 small Granny Smith apple, cored and thinly sliced
- 1/2 cup toasted sliced almonds
- 1/2 cup grated Parmesan cheese

Directions:

1. In a large bowl, combine squash, 2 tablespoons of the olive oil, House Seasoning, and cayenne pepper; toss to coat well.
2. Place squash in air fryer basket, set air fryer temperature to 400 degrees, and cook for 15 minutes, shaking occasionally. Let cool.
3. In a large bowl, whisk together lemon juice, shallot, salt, and remaining olive oil. Add arugula and toss to coat. Divide arugula between 4 salad plates and top with squash and apple slices. Sprinkle with sliced almonds and Parmesan cheese. Serve chilled.

Air Fryer Pigs In A Blanket

Servings: 10
Cooking Time: 8 Minutes

Ingredients:

- 1 can crescent rolls
- 24 cocktail sausages

Directions:

1. Preheat the air fryer to 350 degrees Fahrenheit. Prepare the air fryer basket with nonstick cooking spray, or once the air fryer has been preheated, add parchment paper.
2. Take a pizza cutter and slice each crescent dough sheet into thirds.
3. Take the cut crescent dough and wrap the dough around the sausage.
4. Place the crescent dogs into the prepared air fryer basket in a single layer and make sure to allow an inch or two between each crescent sausage. You may need to cook in batches if needed.
5. Air fry on 350 degrees Fahrenheit for 3-4 minutes, flip, and then air fry for an additional 3-4 minutes, or until the crescents are golden brown.
6. Carefully remove from the air fryer basket and serve with your favorite dipping sauces.

Notes

This recipe was made using the Cosori 5.8 qt air fryer. If you are using a different air fryer, your cook time may need to be adjusted up or down depending on the wattage and power of the heating element.

WHAT DIPPING SAUCES CAN I USE FOR PIGS IN A BLANKET?
I love to use ketchup and mustard, but you can also use bbq sauce, cheese sauce, honey mustard sauce, ranch dressing, and more.
CAN I COOK FROZEN PIGS IN A BLANKET IN THE AIR FRYER?
Absolutely! If you are cooking these pigs in a blanket from frozen, you will want to add a minute or two to the cooking time to ensure they are cooked completely.

Air Fryer Asparagus Salad With Feta Vinaigrette

Servings: 4

Ingredients:

- 1 lb. asparagus
- 2 tbsp. olive oil, divided
- Kosher salt and pepper
- 1 tbsp. rice vinegar
- 1 small shallot, finely chopped
- 1/4 c. fresh mint, finely chopped
- 2 oz. feta, crumbled
- 2 tbsp. fresh dill, roughly chopped

Directions:

1. Heat oven to 425°F. On a small rimmed baking sheet, toss asparagus with 1 tablespoon oil and ¼ teaspoon each salt and pepper. Roast until just tender, 8 to 12 minutes; transfer to platter.
2. Meanwhile, in small bowl, combine vinegar, shallot and ¼ teaspoon each salt and pepper. Let sit, tossing occasionally, until asparagus is done.
3. Stir remaining tablespoon oil into shallot mixture, then gently toss with mint and feta. Spoon over asparagus and sprinkle with dill.
4. AIR FRYING INSTRUCTIONS:
5. Heat air fryer to 400°F. Toss asparagus with 1 tablespoon olive oil and 1/4 teaspoon each salt and pepper. Air-fry, shaking basket halfway through, until tender, 10 minutes. Proceed with steps 2-3.

Crispy Parmesan Potato Wedges

Servings: 2

Ingredients:
- 2 small russet potatoes
- 2 tablespoons (28 grams) Parmesan cheese, grated
- ¾ teaspoon (4 grams) salt
- ¼ teaspoon (2 grams) garlic powder
- ¼ teaspoon (2 grams) paprika
- ¼ teaspoon (2 grams) dried oregano
- 1 tablespoon (15 milliliters) neutral-flavored oil

Directions:
1. Cut each potato lengthwise into 8 wedges and place them in a large bowl.
2. Add the remaining ingredients and toss to coat.
3. Place the crisper plate into the Smart Air Fryer basket, then place the potatoes onto the crisper plate.
4. Select the Fries function, adjust time to 22 minutes, and press Start/Pause.
5. Remove the potato wedges when done and serve.

Air Fryer Roasted Garlic

Servings: 1/2
Cooking Time: 10 Minutes

Ingredients:
- 3 full bulbs garlic
- 1-2 tablespoons olive oil
- 1 teaspoon salt

Directions:
1. Preheat air fryer to 400 F
2. Carefully slice the tops off the garlic bulbs; the cloves inside should be exposed.
3. Drizzle the olive oil over top of each garlic bulb, making sure all the cloves get covered.
4. Sprinkle salt on each bulb and tightly wrap each in tin foil.
5. Place garlic into your air fryer and cook for 18-20 minutes, or until garlic is tender.
6. Allow to cool until you can handle and remove the bulbs from the papery skin.

Air Fryer Garlic Knots

Servings: 6
Cooking Time: 8 Minutes

Ingredients:
- 1 can store-bought pizza dough 13.8 ounces or two cans of thin crust pizza 8 ounces each
- 4 tablespoons unsalted butter melted
- 1/4 cup parmesan cheese grated
- 2 cloves garlic minced
- 1 tablespoon dried parsley flakes
- 1 teaspoon Italian Seasoning

Directions:
1. Open the can of premade pizza dough and on a lightly floured surface, roll it out into a rectangle.
2. With a pizza cutter or kitchen knife cut the dough into twelve 1-inch strips, and then fold each strip in half. Tie each piece into dough knots, making 12 knots.
3. Place the dough balls into the air fryer basket in a single layer, lined with parchment paper, a silicone baking mat or lightly sprayed with olive oil spray.
4. Air fry at 350 degrees F for 8-10 minutes, until they are golden brown.
5. While knots are in a small mixing bowl, stir together the melted butter, parmesan cheese, garlic, parsley flakes, and Italian seasoning.
6. When knots are golden brown, use a pastry brush and generously brush garlic butter on each piece with butter and seasonings and top with grated parmesan cheese.

Notes

Kitchen Tips: Make these in batches without overcrowding the basket. Use a food scale to ensure they are all the same size, so they cook evenly. To get a deeper brown color cook for 1 additional minute.

If using regular crust dough, knots will be just a tad bit thicker and may need 1-2 additional minutes of air frying time.

For smaller bites, just cut the dough in half, and you will have 24 garlic knots.

Optional Favorite Dipping Sauce: Our favorite sauce for dipping is marinara. But you can use other sauces, like homemade marinara sauce, alfredo sauce, pesto sauce, pizza sauce or Greek yogurt with roasted garlic.

Artichoke Wings With Vegan Ranch Dip

Servings: 6

Ingredients:

- Artichoke Wings
- One 16-ounce jar marinated artichoke hearts
- 1½ cups all-purpose flour
- 1 teaspoon garlic powder
- 1 teaspoon onion powder
- 1 teaspoon paprika
- 1 teaspoon kosher salt
- One 12-ounce bottle beer (Lager or Weisse-style for best results)
- 2 cups panko breadcrumbs
- Vegan Ranch Dip
- 1 cup vegan mayonnaise
- ¼ cup non-dairy milk (i.e., coconut, oat, or any nut milk)
- 2 tablespoons fresh dill, finely chopped
- 1 teaspoon fresh Italian parsley leaves, finely chopped
- 1 teaspoon vegan Worcestershire sauce (optional)
- 1 teaspoon apple cider vinegar
- 1 teaspoon lemon juice
- 1 clove garlic, grated
- 1 teaspoon onion powder
- 1 teaspoon black pepper
- Kosher salt, to taste
- Oil spray

Directions:

1. Select the Preheat function on the Air Fryer then press Start/Pause.
2. Drain the artichoke hearts and pat dry with paper towels.
3. Whisk together the flour, garlic powder, onion powder, paprika, and salt in a large bowl until evenly distributed.
4. Pour in the beer and whisk well until no lumps remain. The mixture should resemble pancake batter.
5. Place the panko breadcrumbs in a separate medium bowl.
6. Line the preheated air fryer baskets with parchment paper.
7. Dredge the artichoke hearts in the beer batter, then roll in the panko breadcrumbs.
8. Shake off any excess breadcrumbs, then place the dredged artichoke hearts into the lined air fryer baskets.
9. Spray the wings lightly with oil and insert into the preheated air fryer.
10. Adjust temperature to 400°F and time to 10 minutes, press Shake, then press Start/Pause.
11. Flip the wings and spray again halfway through cooking. The Shake Reminder will let you know when.
12. Combine all the dressing ingredients in a separate medium bowl and whisk together.
13. Season to taste with kosher salt. Pour into a bowl for dipping.
14. Remove the artichoke wings from the air fryer when done.
15. Serve immediately with the vegan ranch dressing.

Air Fryer Sweet Potato Casserole

Servings: 6

Cooking Time: 10 Minutes

Ingredients:

- 29 ounce sweet potato yams drained
- 3/4 cup pecans
- 1/4 teaspoon salt
- 1 egg
- 1/2 teaspoon vanilla extract
- 1/4 teaspoon ground cinnamon
- 1 1/4 cup granulated white sugar

- 1 Tablespoon heavy cream
- 2 Tablespoons unsalted butter softened

Directions:
1. Preheat the air fryer to 350 degrees Fahrenheit.
2. Place the sweet potatoes into a medium sized mixing bowl. Add the salt, butter, egg, vanilla extract, ground cinnamon, white sugar, and heavy cream. Mix thoroughly for one minute.
3. Place the pecans in a food processor. Chop the pecans until they are small and easy to sprinkle.
4. Take the sweet potato mixture and place in a prepared 7" springform pan. Cover the top with the chopped pecans.
5. Place the springform pan into the air fryer basket. Air fry for 10-12 minutes or until the topping is browned.

Notes

Can I make a sweet potato casserole in the air fryer with a marshmallow topping?

Yes, you can, but you may want to consider doing it a little differently than the traditional method of topping the casserole with mini marshmallows. Because marshmallows are light and fluffy, they can easily blow around and possibly blow up into the heating element.If you want to have a marshmallow topping, consider using the jarred marshmallow fluff, or push the marshmallows into the casserole so that they don't fly around while air frying.

How do I store leftover sweet potato casserole?

Store leftover sweet potato casserole in an airtight container in the refrigerator for up to 4 days.

How do I reheat leftover air fryer sweet potato casserole?

To reheat leftover casserole, add it to an oven-safe dish and reheat in the air fryer at 350 degrees Fahrenheit for 2-3 minutes, or until the casserole is heated through.

What are additions I can make to sweet potato casserole?

You can change the flavors in sweet potato casserole by adding different ingredients such as diced pineapple. It gives the casserole an even more pronounced flavor and it is delicious!

Air Fryer Diced Potatoes

Servings: 4
Cooking Time: 20 Minutes

Ingredients:
- 1 ½ pounds of small potatoes
- 2 cups cold water
- 1 tablespoon fresh thyme or 1 teaspoon dried thyme
- ½ tablespoon minced garlic
- ½ tablespoon olive oil
- Juice of 1/2 a lemon, about 2 tablespoons of a medium size lemon
- Salt to taste

Directions:
1. Wash your potatoes and dice them into small cubes. The closer they are in size, the more evenly they will cook.
2. Soak the cut potatoes for 10 minutes in cold water. This will help remove some starch and allow them to crisp up more. Once they have soaked, drain them and then pat them dry with a paper towel.
3. Combine potatoes with the thyme, garlic, olive oil and lemon juice.
4. Place diced potatoes in your air fryer basket. Cook at 380 degrees F for 20 to 25 minutes, giving the basket a good shake at the 10 minute mark.

Notes

OPTIONAL

Sprinkle more fresh thyme to the potatoes before serving or some zest from your lemon, or both!

HOW TO REHEAT DICED POTATOES IN THE AIR FRYER

Preheat the air fryer to 350 degrees F.

Lay the leftover diced potatoes in the air fryer basket in a single layer.

Cook for 3 to 5 minutes until heated through.

Air Fryer Kielbasa

Servings: 4
Cooking Time: 8 Minutes

Ingredients:
- 1 package Kielbasa 15 ounces

Directions:
1. To make this kielbasa dish, remove sausage from packaging, and then cut into bite-size pieces (about ½ inch sized coin size pieces.)
2. Transfer to the air fryer basket, and air fry at 380 degrees F for 8-10 minutes. I tossed the pieces of sausage halfway through air frying.
3. Remove from basket and serve!

Notes

How to Air Fry Frozen Kielbasa

If you want to make this from frozen, place it in the air fryer basket, and air fry at 380 degrees F, for 10-12 minutes cooking time.

halfway through. Once done, top with parmesan cheese and parsley. Salt and pepper to taste.

Air Fryer Fried Pickles

Servings: 4
Cooking Time: 10 Minutes

Ingredients:
- 2 cups dill pickle slices
- 1/2 cup flour
- 1 large egg
- 1 Tablespoon water
- 1/2 cup bread crumbs
- 1/4 cup grated Parmesan
- 1 Tablespoon Italian seasoning

Directions:
1. Lay the pickles on a paper towel and pat dry. In the first small bowl add the flour. In the second small bowl add the egg and whisk with the water. In the last bowl add the bread crumbs, parmesan, and italian seasoning.
2. Dip each pickle in the flour, then the egg and lastly in the bread crumb mixture.
3. Lay the pickles in a single layer in the air fryer basket. Cook at 400 degrees for 8-10 minutes. Serve with your favorite dipping sauce.

Hot Cauliflower Wings

Servings: 4

Ingredients:
- For the wings
- 1/2 head of cauliflower, cut into florets
- 1 cup of flour, you can use gluten free flour
- 1 1/2 cup of coconut milk
- 1/2 tsp smoked paprika powder
- 1/3 tsp harrisa powder
- salt and black pepper
- 1/2 tsp garlic powder
- For the sauce
- 1 cup of bbq sauce
- 2 tbsp sweet and sour sauce
- 2 tbsp tomato puree
- 2 tbsp lemon juice
- 2 tbsp honey
- 1 tbsp sriracha sauce (optional)

Directions:
1. Start by chopping cauliflower to smaller florets.
2. Prepare the batter by placing in the bowl; coconut milk, spices, salt & pepper and flour. Mix until everything is well incorporated.
3. Preheat your ninja electric grill on air frying mode to 200C.
4. Coat each cauliflower floret in the batter. Shake off the excess of the batter.
5. Place them in the air fryer cooking basket, don't place them to close together, as they will stick.
6. Once that's done, set the time to 10 min. Shake the florets half way the time, make sure they crisp evenly on both sides.
7. Make the sauce by placing all ingredients in the small pot. Cook for 5-7 min on a medium heat steering. The sauce should thicken a bit.
8. Coat each baked cauliflower florets in the sauce.
9. Serve hot.

Easy Air Fryer Radishes

Servings: 2
Cooking Time: 7 Minutes

Ingredients:
- 2 cups radishes
- 1 tablespoon olive oil
- ½ teaspoon garlic powder
- ½ teaspoon onion powder
- salt and pepper to taste

Directions:
1. Preheat air fryer to 400°F.
2. Wash, trim and dry radishes.
3. Cut into quarters, then toss with oil and seasonings until evenly coated.
4. Cook radishes for 7-8 minutes or until crisp and tender, or to your liking.

Air Fryer Mushrooms

Servings: 4

Cooking Time: 7 Minutes

Ingredients:
- 16 ounces button mushrooms halved
- 1 clove garlic minced
- 1 tablespoon olive oil
- 1 1/2 tablespoons butter
- 1 tablespoon soy sauce
- 1/2 teaspoon salt
- 1/2 teaspoon pepper
- 1/2 teaspoon garlic powder

Directions:
1. Preheat the air fryer to 180C/350F. Grease an air fryer basket.
2. In a mixing bowl, add all the ingredients and mix well.
3. Transfer the mushrooms to the air fryer basket and cook for 7-8 minutes, shaking halfway through.
4. Remove the mushrooms from the air fryer and sprinkle with fresh parsley.

Notes

TO STORE: Despite their delicate nature, they can still be stored in your fridge for up to 24 hours by placing them in airtight containers.

TO FREEZE: Place the cooked and cooled mushrooms in a shallow container and store them in the freezer for up to one month.

TO REHEAT: Either microwave them for 20-30 seconds or reheat them back up in the air fryer.

Air Fryer Tofu

Servings: 4

Cooking Time: 10 Minutes

Ingredients:
- 15 oz tofu extra firm
- 1/2 tablespoon olive oil
- 1/2 tablespoon sesame oil
- 2 tablespoons soy sauce
- 1/2 teaspoon garlic powder
- 1/2 teaspoon ground ginger
- 1/4 teaspoon salt

Directions:
1. Preheat the air fryer to 190C/375F.
2. Cube the tofu into bite sizes pieces. Place the tofu on a dishtowel or paper towel to soak up excess moisture.
3. In a large bowl, combine the olive oil, sesame oil, soy sauce, garlic powder, and salt. Add the tofu and mix well, until all the tofu is coated.
4. Generously grease the air fryer basket and add a single layer of tofu to it. Air fry for 10-12 minutes, shaking the basket several times throughout.
5. Once the tofu is golden brown, remove it from the basket and repeat the process until all the tofu is cooked up.

Notes

TO STORE: Store leftover crispy tofu in an airtight container in the fridge for up to 4 days.

TO REHEAT: To reheat air-fried tofu, preheat the air fryer to 375F degrees. Add tofu to the air fryer basket and cook for a few minutes until heated through.

TO FREEZE: You can also freeze air-fried tofu if you have made a big batch. Flash-freeze tofu and transfer it into an airtight bag or container. Keep cooked tofu in the freezer for up to 3 months.

Maple Glazed Roasted Vegetables With Pesto And Spiced Nuts

Servings: 4

Cooking Time: 40 Minutes

Ingredients:
- For the vegetables
- 500 g carrots, sliced lengthways then into diagonal chunks (or so evenly sized)
- 500 g parsnips, sliced lengthways then into diagonal chunks (or so evenly sized)
- 200 g brussels sprouts
- 1 red onion
- 2 cloves of garlic, minced
- 4 tbsp maple syrup

- 1 tbsp wholegrain mustard
- 150 g mixed nuts
- 2 tbsp olive oil
- 1 sprig fresh rosemary,
- 1 tsp cayenne
- For the pesto
- 50 g fresh basil leaves
- 2 cloves of garlic, crushed
- 25 g pine nuts
- 40 parmesan, grated
- 4 tbsp olive oil

Directions:
1. For the vegetables
2. In a large bowl, whisk together the 3 tbsp of maple syrup, mustard and 1 tbsp of the olive oil
3. Pre-heat the air fryer to 190 degrees
4. Add the veg to the maple marinade and toss together so all the pieces are coated.
5. Place veggie pieces into the air fryer tray and cook for 15/20 minutes – you may need to do this in batches, around half way through give the air fryer pan a shake or 2 to give an even cook
6. For the pesto
7. Put the basil leaves in a food processor with the garlic and pine nuts Blitz for a few seconds, then add the cheese and oil and blitz again until you have a spoon-able paste.
8. For the nuts
9. Preheat air fryer to 150 degrees
10. In a bowl add the rosemary, cayenne, 1 tbsp oil, 1 tbsp of maple syrup, and the nuts
11. Mix together so all the nuts are coated.
12. Add to tray of the air fryer in one layer and air fry for around 5-8 minutes – about half way give the tray a shake.
13. Once cool, arrange the dish of the veggies, drizzle of pesto and a sprinkling of the spiced nuts – and serve up!

Air Fryer Totchos

Servings: 4

Ingredients:
- 2 lb. frozen potato tots
- 1 tsp. chili powder
- 1/2 tsp. ground cumin
- 1/2 tsp. ground coriander
- 1/8 tsp. cayenne
- 1 1/2 c. finely grated extra-sharp Cheddar cheese

Directions:
1. Toss tots with chili powder, cumin, coriander, and cayenne. Heat air fryer to 400°F. Arrange tots in single layer in air fryer basket and cook 20 minutes.
2. Transfer half of tots to small platter and sprinkle with half of Cheddar. Top with remaining tots and cheese, then cover loosely with aluminum foil for about 30 seconds to melt cheese. Serve immediately.

Air-fried Buffalo Cauliflower

Servings: 2

Cooking Time: 10 Minutes

Ingredients:
- 1 2.25 pound head cauliflower, trimmed and broken into florets
- ¼ cup bottled cayenne pepper sauce (such as Frank's Red Hot®)
- 2 tablespoon melted butter
- 2 teaspoon vinegar
- ⅛ teaspoon garlic powder
- Kosher salt (optional)
- Thinly sliced green onions (optional)
- Purchased blue cheese dip or salad dressing

Directions:
1. Preheat air fryer to 400° F, according to manufacturer's directions.
2. In a large bowl, combine cauliflower, hot sauce, butter, vinegar, and garlic powder. Transfer half of the cauliflower to the air fryer basket and cook 10 to 12 minutes, shaking the basket every 5 minutes.

Keep warm on a baking sheet in a 200°F. oven while frying remaining cauliflower. Sprinkle with kosher salt and green onions before serving, if desired. Serve with blue cheese dip.

Crispy Air Fryer Brussels Sprouts

Ingredients:
- 1 lb. brussels sprouts, trimmed and halved lengthwise (approximately 4 cups)
- 1 tablespoon olive oil
- 1/2 tablespoon Italian seasoning
- 1/2 tablespoon garlic powder
- 1/8 teaspoon salt
- 1/4 teaspoon ground black pepper, or to taste

Directions:
1. Combine all ingredients in a large bowl and toss to combine and coat brussels sprouts evenly. Transfer brussels sprouts to air fryer basket.
2. Turn air fryer on to 350 F and cook for 12 minutes, until brussels sprouts are cooked through and golden brown on the edges.

Notes
These instructions work best with a Philips Air Fryer (1.8 lb/2.75 qt). If you have larger or smaller air fryer, you will have to adjust the cook time. Just check in on the brussels sprouts every 5 minutes to make sure that it cooks through and that they don't burn.

Air Fryer Buffalo Cauliflower

Servings: 6
Cooking Time: 12 Minutes

Ingredients:
- 1 head cauliflower cut into bite-sized pieces
- 1 cup buffalo sauce Frank's or preferred brand
- 2 tablespoons olive oil
- ½ teaspoon seasoned salt
- ½ teaspoon garlic powder

Directions:
1. Preheat air fryer to 370°F.
2. Cut cauliflower into bite-sized pieces.
3. Combine all ingredients in a large bowl and mix until cauliflower is evenly coated.
4. Place cauliflower in the air fryer basket and cook for 12-15 minutes or until the cauliflower is crispy.

Notes
Store leftovers in the refrigerator for 3-5 days. To reheat, place in a 370°F air fryer and heat until steaming hot.

Air Fryer Chili Garlic Tofu

Servings: 5
Cooking Time: 15 Minutes

Ingredients:
- 1 package super firm tofu
- 1/2 cup cornstarch, arrowroot, or tapioca
- 1 tablespoon olive oil
- 1/4 cup low-sodium soy sauce
- 2 tablespoons chili garlic sauce
- 1 tablespoon rice vinegar
- 1 1/2 tablespoons swerve or brown sugar
- 2 garlic cloves, minced
- 1 teaspoon grated fresh ginger
- 1 teaspoon sesame oil
- 1/2 teaspoon toasted sesame seeds
- 2 green onions, sliced

Directions:
1. Wrap tofu in multiple layers of paper towels. Place a cast iron pan or something heavy on top. Let sit for 30 minutes. Or you can use a tofu press.
2. Cut tofu into cubes.
3. Place cornstarch in a large zip top bag. Shake to coat. Remove tofu pieces, shaking off excess and place in a medium bowl. Drizzle with 1 tablespoon olive oil and gently toss.
4. Place half the tofu pieces in the Air Fryer basket. Set to 370 for 15 minutes. Halfway through open. If they still look powdery, spray them with a little olive oil.
5. Check after about 12 minutes. The cooking time is just an estimate and can vary based on Air Fryer model and size of cubes and brand of tofu.

6. Remove tofu from Air Fryer and set aside. Repeat with remaining tofu.
7. In a nonstick skillet, combine soy sauce, chili garlic sauce, vinegar, sverve, garlic, and ginger. Bring to a boil and simmer for 1 minute.
8. Add sesame oil and tofu and cook and stir for 1 minute.
9. Sprinkle with sesame seeds and green onions.

Notes

Use gluten-free soy sauce to make this recipe gluten-free.

Mexican Street Corn

Servings: 4
Cooking Time: 12 Minutes

Ingredients:

- 4 ears corn, husks and silks removed
- 1 cup Mexican crema
- 2 limes, zested and juiced
- ½ cup cotija cheese, finely crumbled
- ⅓ cup cilantro, finely chopped
- 2 tablespoons chile de arbol powder or other chili powder
- Items Needed:
- Empty squeeze bottle with lid
- Funnel (optional)

Directions:

1. Place the cooking pot into the base of the Smart Indoor Grill, followed by the grill grate.
2. Select the Air Grill function on max heat, adjust time to 12 minutes, press Shake, then press Start/Pause to preheat.
3. Place the corn onto the preheated grill grate, then close the lid.
4. Flip the corn halfway through cooking. The Shake Reminder will let you know when.
5. Place the crema and lime juice in a medium bowl and stir until well combined, then transfer into the squeeze bottle. Place the cap onto the squeeze bottle and then set aside until ready to use.
6. Note: Using a funnel may help transferring the crema to the squeeze bottle. Remove the corn when done and place onto a platter.
7. Use the squeeze bottle to apply the crema to the top of the corn, then sprinkle the lime zest, cotija cheese, cilantro, and chile powder over the top and serve.

Air Fryer Herbed Brussels Sprouts

Servings: 4
Cooking Time: 8 Minutes

Ingredients:

- 1 lb. brussels sprouts (cleaned and trimmed)
- ½ tsp. dried thyme
- 1 tsp. dried parsley
- 1 tsp. garlic powder (Or 4 cloves, minced)
- ¼ tsp. salt
- 2 tsp. oil

Directions:

1. Remove any outer leaves of the brussels sprouts that don't look healthy. Lightly cook your brussels sprouts, either by boiling them for 13-15 minutes or by microwaving them on high for about 3-4 minutes.
2. Cut them in half.
3. Place all ingredients in a medium or large mixing bowl and toss to coat the brussels sprouts evenly.
4. Pour them into the food basket of the air fryer and close it up.
5. Set the heat to 390 F. and the time to 8 minutes. This setting roasts them nicely on the outside while leaving the insides a nicely cooked al dente.
6. Cool slightly and serve.

Notes

Please note that the nutrition data below is a ballpark figure. Exact data is not possible.

Air Fryer Twice-baked Potatoes

Ingredients:
- 1 medium baking potato
- 1 Tbsp olive oil
- Salt & pepper
- 1 Tbsp butter, softened
- ½ Tbsp 2% milk
- 1.5 oz cream cheese
- 1 Tbsp sour cream
- Green onions (optional)

Directions:
1. Pierce potato and brush lightly with olive oil. Sprinkle outside with salt and pepper.
2. Bake in your air fryer for 15 minutes at 400°F. Flip and bake for 15 additional minutes.
3. Set aside potato to cool. When cool enough to handle, cut in half lengthwise, then scoop out pulp, leaving a thin shell.
4. In a small bowl, mash the pulp with butter, milk, and a pinch of salt. Stir in cream cheese and sour cream. Spoon into potato shells.
5. Return potatoes to air fryer. Bake, uncovered, until heated through and the tops are golden brown, approximately 15 minutes. Top with sliced green onions, if desired. Enjoy!

Air Fryer Roasted Rainbow Carrots

Servings: 4
Cooking Time: 6 Minutes

Ingredients:
- ½ pound tri-color carrots 1 inch pieces
- 1 tablespoon olive oil
- 1 tablespoon honey
- salt and pepper to taste

Directions:
1. Preheat the air fryer to 400°F.
2. Toss the carrots with the remaining ingredients until fully coated.
3. Place carrots in the air fryer basket and cook for 7-8 minutes and serve.

Air-fryer Crispy Tofu Recipe

Servings: 2
Cooking Time: 17 Minutes

Ingredients:
- 280g pack The Tofoo Co extra firm tofu, drained and cut into 1-2cm cubes
- 1 tbsp cornflour
- ¼ tsp white pepper
- pinch chilli flakes
- 1 tsp sesame seeds
- 1 tsp vegetable oil
- chopped fresh coriander, to serve (optional)
- chopped fresh coriander, to serve (optional)
- 1 tbsp runny honey
- 1 tsp rice wine vinegar
- 1 clove garlic, crushed

Directions:
1. Preheat the air-fryer to 200°C.
2. Pat dry the drained tofu and put into a bowl. Sprinkle over the cornflour, white pepper, chilli flakes and sesame seeds and season with salt and black pepper. Toss well until coated, then drizzle over the oil, tossing to coat.
3. Put the tofu pieces into the air-fryer, well-spaced. Cook for 15 mins, shaking every 5 mins, until golden and very crisp.
4. For the sauce, put all the ingredients into a heat-safe bowl and microwave for 1-2 mins, stirring regularly, until steaming. Mix well and set aside to cool. Serve alongside the crispy tofu bites or drizzle over and toss to glaze if you prefer.

Air Fryer Mushrooms And Onions

Servings: 2

Ingredients:
- 2 cloves garlic, minced
- 2 tbsp. extra-virgin olive oil
- 4 tsp. fresh lemon juice, plus 1/4 tsp. finely grated lemon zest for serving
- 1 tsp. kosher salt

- 1 tsp. Worcestershire sauce
- 1 lb. baby bella or button mushrooms, halved, quartered if large
- 1 small yellow onion, halved and thinly sliced
- 1 tbsp. chopped fresh parsley
- 1 tbsp. fresh thyme leaves

Directions:
1. In a large heatproof bowl, whisk garlic, oil, lemon juice, salt, and Worcestershire to combine. Add mushrooms and onion and toss until oil mixture is completely absorbed by mushrooms (this will take about 30 seconds).
2. Working in batches if necessary, in an air-fryer basket, spoon mushroom mixture in a single layer; reserve bowl. Cook at 400°, tossing a few times to ensure even cooking, until mushrooms and onions are tender and golden, 13 to 15 minutes.
3. Return hot mushroom mixture to reserved bowl. Toss with parsley, thyme, and lemon zest.

Air Fryer Baked Potato

Servings: 1
Cooking Time: 30 Minutes-1 Hour

Ingredients:
- 1 baking potato (see recipe tips and weigh before cooking), scrubbed and dried
- light rapeseed, vegetable or sunflower oil
- salt and freshly ground black pepper
- For the cheddar and jalapeño topping
- small handful grated cheddar
- 1 ripe tomato, diced
- few green jalapeño pepper slices from a jar
- For the smashed avocado topping
- 1 small, ripe avocado (or a few frozen avocado slices)
- ½ lime or lemon, juice only
- handful mixed seeds, dukkah, za'atar or chilli flakes
- For the curried beans topping
- 227g tin baked beans
- ½ tsp curry powder
- natural yoghurt and lime pickle (optional), to serve

Directions:
1. Rub the potato all over with a little oil. If you like, rub a little salt over the skin – this will help give a crispier finish.
2. Put the potato in the air fryer and turn to 200C (you don't want to preheat, to avoid burning the skin before the inside is cooked.) Air-fry for 20 minutes, then turn the potato over. A small potato will take another 20 minutes or so, a large one another 25–30 minutes.
3. Check the middle is soft by poking a table knife into the centre – it should slide in easily. If it's not quite done, continue to cook for a minute at a time.
4. For the cheddar and jalapeño topping, mix the cheese, tomato and jalapeño slices, split the potato and spoon the cheese mixture on top.
5. For the smashed avocado topping, mash the avocado with the lime or lemon juice, salt and pepper. Split the potato, spoon in the avocado mixture and scatter with the seeds or your choice of seasoning.
6. For the curried beans topping, heat the beans with the curry powder until hot but not boiling. Split the potato and pile on the beans. Top with dollops of yoghurt and lime pickle, if using.

Notes
Small potatoes, around 225g/8oz each, will be ready in 40 minutes. Large potatoes, around 350g/12oz each, will take 45–50 minutes to get soft inside.
You can speed up the cooking by microwaving your jacket potatoes first. Microwave on high power for four minutes, turn the potato over, and microwave for another four minutes. (If you are cooking two potatoes, you may need to microwave them for an extra 2 minutes.) Then cook in the air-fryer for 10 minutes to crisp up.
Look for potatoes labelled as bakers, or a floury variety, such as King Edward, Maris Piper, Vivaldi or Estima.

FAVORITE AIR FRYER RECIPES

Air Fryer Bagel Pizzas

Servings: 2
Cooking Time: 10 Minutes

Ingredients:
- 1 bagel, split in half
- 1/2 cup (120 ml) pizza sauce or tomato sauce
- 1/3 cup (40 g) shredded cheese
- salt, to taste
- black pepper, to taste
- OPTIONAL TOPPINGS
- Pepperoni, cooked Sausage, Bacon pieces, diced Ham, sliced or diced Tomatoes, Mushrooms, Pineapple, etc.
- OTHER SAUCE OPTIONS
- BBQ Sauce, Salsa, White (Alfredo) Sauce, Pesto, etc.
- EQUIPMENT
- Air Fryer
- Air Fryer Rack optional
- Oil Sprayer optional

Directions:
1. Cut the bagels in half and place each half in the air fryer, cut side down (if air frying multiple bagels, only cook in a single layer - cook in batches if needed). Air Fry at 360°F/182°C for 2 minutes.
2. Flip the bagels halves to cut side up. Continue to Air Fry at 360°F/182°C for another 1-2 minutes (if you want the crusts extra crispy - air fry each side an additional minute or two more).
3. Add sauce, toppings, and cheese on top of the bagel halves. Lightly spray with oil for extra crispy.
4. Cover toppings with an air fryer rack to keep toppings from flying around.
5. Air Fry 360°F/182°C for 2-4 minutes or until heated through and cheese is melted. Try air frying for about 2 minutes first. If you want the top to be crispier, add additional minute or two until the bagel pizzas are crispy and cheese is melted.
6. Allow to cool for about 2 minutes. Serve warm.

Air Fryer Taco Calzones

Servings: 4
Cooking Time: 10 Minutes

Ingredients:
- 1 tube Pillsbury thin crust pizza dough
- 1 cup taco meat
- 1 cup shredded cheddar

Directions:
1. Spread out your sheet of pizza dough on a clean surface. Using a pizza cutter, cut the dough into 4 even squares.
2. Cut each square into a large circle using the pizza cutter. Set the dough scraps aside to make cinnamon sugar bites.
3. Top one half of each circle of dough with 1/4 cup taco meat and 1/4 cup shredded cheese.
4. Fold the empty half over the meat and cheese and press the edges of the dough together with a fork to seal it tightly. Repeat with all four calzones.
5. Gently pick up each calzone and spray it with pan spray or olive oil. Arrange them in your Air Fryer basket.
6. Cook the calzones at 325° for 8-10 minutes. Watch them closely at the 8 minute mark so you don't overcook them.
7. Serve with salsa and sour cream.
8. To make cinnamon sugar bites, cut the scraps of dough into even sized pieces, about 2 inches long. Add them to the Air Fryer basket and cook at 325° for 5 minutes. Immediately toss with 1:4 cinnamon sugar mixture.

Air Fryer Hot Dogs

Servings: 4
Cooking Time: 8 Minutes

Ingredients:
- 4 hot dogs
- 4 hot dog buns
- Optional toppings: ketchup, relish, mustard, chopped onions

Directions:
1. Heat an air fryer to 375°F.
2. Place 4 hot dogs in a single layer in the air fryer basket. Air fry until the hot dogs look plump and are slightly browned, flipping them halfway through, 5 to 6 minutes total.
3. If you want toasted buns, transfer a hot dog into each bun. Return to the air fryer basket in a single layer and air fry until the buns are toasted, about 2 minutes. Serve with desired toppings.

Air Fryer Frozen Corn Dogs

Servings: 5
Cooking Time: 10 Minutes

Ingredients:
- 5 frozen corn dogs

Directions:
1. Preheat your air fryer to 350 degrees.
2. Place the frozen corn dogs into the air fryer and cook for 10-13 minutes, checking the inside with an Instant Read Thermometer.
3. Remove the corn dogs from the air fryer and enjoy!

Notes

HOW TO REHEAT CORN DOGS IN AN AIR FRYER:
Preheat your air fryer to 400 degrees.
Cook the corn dogs in the air fryer for 3-5 minutes, remove them from the air fryer, and enjoy!

Air Fryer Tostones

Servings: 2
Cooking Time: 20 Minutes

Ingredients:
- 1 large green plantain (ends trimmed and peeled (6 oz after))
- olive oil spray (I like Bertolli)
- 1 cup water
- 1 teaspoon kosher salt
- 3/4 teaspoon garlic powder

Directions:
1. With a sharp knife cut a slit along the length of the plantain skin, this will make it easier to peel. Cut the plantain into 1 inch pieces, 8 total.
2. In a small bowl combine the water with salt and garlic powder.
3. Preheat the air fryer to 400F.
4. When ready, spritz the plantain with olive oil and cook 6 minutes, you might have to do this in 2 batches.
5. Remove from the air fryer and while they are hot mash them with a tostonera or the bottom of a jar or measuring cup to flatten.
6. Dip them in the seasoned water and set aside.
7. Preheat the air fryer to 400F once again and cook, in batches 5 minutes on each side, spraying both sides of the plantains with olive oil.
8. When done, give them another spritz of oil and season with salt. Eat right away.

Air Fried Spicy Duck Leg

Servings: 4

Ingredients:
- 2 duck legs
- For the marinade
- 1 orange, juiced
- 1/2 tsp fresh ginger
- 1 tsp granulated garlic
- 4 tbsp olive oil
- Chilli powder, as much as you like

- Salt and pepper
- COOKING MODE
- When entering cooking mode - We will enable your screen to stay 'always on' to avoid any unnecessary interruptions whilst you cook!

Directions:
1. Combine all marinate ingredients.
2. Coat duck leg everywhere with the marinate and leave in in the fridge, in air tight container for at least 2-4h to marinate.
3. Set ninja health grill on air frying mode, 180 C for 25 min
4. Turn duck leg every 7-10min.
5. Serve with salad and grilled potatoes.

Air Fryer Sausage Rolls

Servings: 12
Cooking Time: 10 Minutes

Ingredients:
- Air Fryer Sausage Rolls
- 3 sausages Note 1
- 3 sheets puff pastry
- 1 tbsp sesame seeds
- 1 eggs

Directions:
1. Air Fryer Sausage Rolls
2. Turn the air fryer on to 180°C/350 F for 15 mins
3. Use a knife and chopping board to remove the casing from the sausages
4. Add egg to a small bowl, pierce yoke and whisk
5. Place a sheet of puff pastry (thawed) onto the chopping board and place 1 off the sausages on top
6. Roll the pastry around the sausage, then use a pastry brush to coat the top of the pastry where the 2 bits of pastry will meet
7. Continue to roll the pastry around the sausage and again brush one side of where the pastry joins with the egg
8. Repeat for each sausage
9. Brush the top of the length of the long rolled sausage with egg
10. Sprinkle the top with sesame seeds
11. Use a knife to cut the excess pastry off each end
12. Then cut the long sausage roll into 4 smaller rolls
13. Spray the Air Fryer Basket with oil (or use baking paper) then place raw sausage rolls into Air Fryer (work in batches)
14. Cook sausage rolls in Air Fryer for 7- 9 mins until pastry is golden and crispy
15. Serve with sauce

Air Fryer Spaghetti Squash

Servings: 4
Cooking Time: 35 Minutes

Ingredients:
- 1 medium spaghetti squash about 3 pounds
- 1 tablespoon olive oil
- ½ teaspoon kosher salt
- ¼ teaspoon black pepper

Directions:
1. Preheat the air fryer to 370°F.
2. Cut the spaghetti squash in half lengthwise. Scoop out the seeds and discard (or save for roasting).
3. Brush the cut side of the squash with oil and season with salt & pepper.
4. Place cut side up in the air fryer and cook 25-30 minutes or until tender and the strands separate easily with a fork.
5. Once cooked, run a fork along the strands of the squash to separate.
6. Toss with butter if desired or season with additional salt and pepper.

Notes

Spaghetti squash seeds can be saved and cooked like pumpkin seeds.

Cook time can vary slightly based on the size of the squash.

Once the strands are separated, they can be topped with your favorite meat sauce and placed back into the squash shells. Top them with mozzarella cheese and air fryer until browned and bubbly.

Keep leftovers in the fridge for up to 3 days. Freeze leftovers in zippered bags for up to 6 months. Let thaw at room temperature before using.

Air Fryer Elote

Servings: 4
Cooking Time: 10 Minutes

Ingredients:
- Corn
- 4 ears of corn on the cob shucked and cleaned
- 2 tablespoons olive oil separated
- 1/2 teaspoon salt separated
- 1/2 teaspoon ground black pepper
- Elote Sauce
- ½ cup plain Greek yogurt
- 2 tablespoons mayo
- 2 oz. cotija cheese crumbled
- 1 tablespoon fresh lime juice
- 1 tablespoon lime zest
- ¼ teaspoon cayenne pepper

Directions:
1. Preheat the air fryer to 350°F. Drizzle the 4 ears of corn with 1 tablespoon of olive oil. Massage the oil into the corn with your hands. Season the corn with ½ teaspoon of salt and ½ teaspoon of pepper.
2. Add 1 tablespoon of olive oil to the bottom of the air fryer and then transfer the corn to the air fryer. Cook the corn for 10 minutes, flipping halfway.
3. While the corn is cooking, add all of the ingredients (except for the cayenne pepper) for the elote sauce to a bowl and mix to combine. Pour the sauce on a large plate. Spread the sauce out evenly.
4. Remove the corn from the air fryer and roll each ear of corn in the elote sauce. Use a spoon to drizzle more elote sauce over the corn. Then season the corn with the cayenne pepper. Enjoy!
5. Air fryer elote on a plate.

Tips & Notes
Every air fryer is different, so the cook time may vary slightly.

If cayenne pepper is too spicy, replace it with ground paprika.

Air Fryer Reheating Leftover Pizza

Servings: 1
Cooking Time: 6 Minutes

Ingredients:
- 1-2 slices leftover pizza
- oil spray , (optional to lightly coat the pizza so toppings don't dry out - need depends on yoout particular toppings)
- EQUIPMENT
- Air Fryer

Directions:
1. Place foil or perforated parchment sheet to base on air fryer basket, rack or tray. Place the pizza on top. If needed, lightly spray the top of pizza so that the toppings don't burn or dry out (optional).
2. Air Fry at 360°F/180°C for 3-6 minutes or until cooked to your desired crispness. If unsure, start cooking for 3 minutes first. Then check to see if it's to your liking. Cook additional minute or two if you want the pizza to be crispier. Deep dish crusts will take a little longer, while thin crust will be slightly quicker.
3. Let the slice of pizza cool for a touch & enjoy!

Notes
Air Frying Tips and Notes:

Recipe timing is based on a non-preheated air fryer. If cooking in multiple slices back to back, the following slices may cook a little quicker because the air fryer is already hot.

Recipes were tested in 3.7 to 6 qt. air fryers. If using a larger air fryer, the pizza slices might cook quicker so adjust cooking time.

Air Fryer Corn Dogs

Servings: 5

Cooking Time: 9 Minutes

Ingredients:
- 5 Corn Dogs

Directions:
1. How To Make Regular Sized Frozen Corn Dogs in the Air Fryer
2. Preheat Air Fryer to 380 degrees Fahrenheit. Prepare the Air Fryer basket with olive oil cooking spray or parchment paper.
3. Place the corn dogs in Air Fryer Basket.
4. Set the cook time to 9 minutes. After 5 minutes, flip the corn dogs in the Air Fryer Basket and then cook for the remainder of time.
5. Serve with your favorite condiments and side items.
6. How To Make Mini Sized Frozen Corn Dogs in the Air Fryer
7. Preheat Air Fryer to 380 degrees Fahrenheit. Prepare the basket with cooking spray or parchment paper.
8. Place the corn dogs in preheated Air Fryer Basket. Be sure to line them up in a single layer.
9. Set the cooking time to 7 minutes. After 4 minutes, flip the mini corn dogs and cook for the remainder of the time.
10. Serve with your favorite condiments or side items.

Notes

It is best to preheat the Air Fryer before making any of your recipes, including frozen corn dogs.

If you're not preheating the Air Fryer cook time will be different. You won't get the same results and your foods may not be cooked thoroughly through.

Just as you would preheat the oven, you want to preheat the Air Fryer as well so that you can ensure you have fully cooked food and that you are also using the correct cook time.

Air Fryer French Bread Pizzas

Servings: 2

Cooking Time: 10 Minutes

Ingredients:
- 1 French bread loaf
- 1/2 cup (120 ml) pizza sauce or tomato sauce
- 1/3 cup (40 g) shredded cheese
- salt , to taste
- black pepper , to taste
- OPTIONAL TOPPINGS
- Pepperoni, cooked Sausage, Bacon pieces, diced Ham, sliced or diced Tomatoes, Mushrooms, Pineapple, etc.
- OTHER SAUCE OPTIONS
- BBQ Sauce, Salsa, White (Alfredo) Sauce, Pesto, etc.
- EQUIPMENT
- Air Fryer
- Air Fryer Rack optional

Directions:
1. Cut French bread loaf to fit the length of your air fryer. Slice in half lengthwise.
2. Lightly spray both sides for an extra crispy crust. Place in air fryer basket/tray with the bottom (crust) side up (only cook in a single layer - cook the pizzas in batches if needed). Air Fry at 360°F/182°C about 2 minutes.
3. Flip the bread, add sauce & toppings.
4. Cover toppings with an air fryer rack to keep toppings from flying around.
5. Air Fry 360°F/182°C for 2-4 minutes or until heated through and cheese is melted. Try air frying for about 2 minutes first. If you want the top to be crispier, add additional minute or two until the pizza is crispy and cheese is melted.
6. Allow pizza to cool for about 2 minutes. Serve warm.

Air Fryer Jalepeno Poppers

Servings: 6
Cooking Time: 12 Minutes

Ingredients:
- 6 medium Jalapeños
- 4 ounces cream cheese, softened
- 6-12 slices bacon

Directions:
1. Cut the jalapeños in half, lengthwise. Remove all of the seeds and rinse the jalapeños.
2. Cut small slices of the cream cheese, in strips, and place a strip inside each half piece of the pepper.
3. Wrap a piece of bacon around the stuffed pepper and secure with a toothpick.
4. Place the stuffed peppers in the basket of the air fryer, working in batches if necessary. Be sure they aren't overlapping each other in the basket.
5. Cook at 370 degrees Fahrenheit for 10-12 minutes, until the bacon is cooked to your desired crispness.

Notes
If you use smaller jalapeños, cut the bacon slices in half before wrapping the pepper.
If the cream cheese is chilled, it is easier to cut into strips.
This recipe makes 12 poppers, with a serving of three poppers per person.

Air Fryer Fried Rice

Ingredients:
- 3 cups rice cooked and cold
- 1 cup frozen mixed vegetables
- 1 tbsp oyster sauce
- 1 tsp sesame oil
- 2 eggs scrambled
- 2 tbsp choppled green onion tops

Directions:
1. To make your air fryer fried rice, put your cold rice into an large bowl.
2. Mix in the frozen vegetables to the bowl of rice.
3. Add the scrambled eggs into the rice and vegetables.
4. Add the sesame oil and oyster sauce. Mix well until fully combined.
5. Transfer the rice mixture to an oven safe container like a ramekin.
6. Place that container into your air fryer. Cook the air fried rice at 360 degrees F for 15 minutes stirring every 5 minutes. Add in the green onion tops during the last minutes of cooking time, stirring them in until well combined.
7. Serve immediately.

Air Fryer Pizza

Servings: 2

Ingredients:
- 2 (8-oz.) packages pizza dough
- 1 tbsp. extra virgin olive oil, divided
- 1/3 c. crushed tomatoes
- 1 clove garlic, minced
- 1/2 tsp. oregano
- Kosher salt
- Freshly ground black pepper
- 1/2 (8-oz.) mozzarella ball, cut into ¼" slices
- Basil leaves, for serving

Directions:
1. On a clean, floured surface, gently flatten ball of dough with your hands until about 8" in diameter (or roughly smaller than your air fryer basket). Repeat with second dough ball. Brush both with olive oil and transfer one, oil side up, into the basket of your air fryer.
2. In a medium bowl, stir to combine crushed tomatoes, garlic, and oregano, and season with salt and pepper. Spoon half tomato mixture onto the center of rolled out pizza dough, then spread into an even layer, leaving ½" outer crust bare.
3. Add half the mozzarella slices to pizza. Air fry on 400° for 10 to 12 minutes, or until crust is golden and cheese is melted.

4. Remove first pizza from air fryer basket using 2 pairs of tongs, and garnish with basil leaves. Assemble and cook second pizza, garnish, and serve.

Air Fryer Bratwurst

Servings: 5
Cooking Time: 15 Minutes

Ingredients:
- 1 pound uncooked bratwurst
- 5 hoagie rolls optional
- toppings for serving dijon mustard, sauerkraut, pickles, etc

Directions:
1. Preheat the air fryer to 360°F.
2. Place the brats in a single layer in the air fryer basket.
3. Cook them for 8 minutes, then flip and cook for an additional 5-6 minutes or until they reach an internal temperature of 165°F.
4. Serve in rolls and/or with desired toppings.

Notes
Ensure brats reach an internal temperature of 165°F.
Do not pierce the brats before cooking or they will lose their juices. Use caution when checking the temperature, they can squirt hot liquid when pierced.
Allow brats to cool for a few minutes before serving or topping.
Nutrition: al information is for brats only and does not include toppings or buns. Information is an estimate and will vary based on brands.
Store leftovers in an airtight container in the fridge for up to 3 days.
Reheat leftovers in the air fryer for up to 5 minutes or until heated through.
Leftovers are great added to pasta or pizza.

Air Fryer Nuts And Bolts

Servings: 4
Cooking Time: 25 Minutes

Ingredients:
- 2 cups dried farfalle pasta
- 60ml (1/4 cup) extra virgin olive oil
- 2 tbsp brown sugar
- 2 tsp smoked paprika
- 1 tsp onion powder
- 1/2 tsp garlic powder
- 1/2 tsp chilli powder
- 1 cup pretzels
- 80g (1/2 cup) raw macadamias
- 80g (1/2 cup) raw cashews
- 1 cup Kellog's Nutri-grain cereal
- 1 tsp sea salt
- Select all ingredients

Directions:
1. Cook pasta in a large saucepan of boiling salted water until just tender. Drain well. Transfer to a tray. Pat dry with paper towel. Transfer to a large bowl.
2. Combine oil, sugar, paprika, onion, garlic and chilli powders in a small bowl. Spoon half of the mixture over pasta. Toss to coat.
3. Preheat air fryer on 200C. Place pasta in air fryer basket. Cook for 5 minutes. Shake basket. Cook for a further 5-6 minutes or until golden and crisp. Transfer to a large bowl.
4. Place pretzels and nuts in a bowl. Add remaining spice mixture. Toss to coat. Place in air fryer basket. Cook on 180C for 3 minutes. Shake basket. Cook for a further 2-3 minutes or until golden. Add to pasta, then add cereal. Sprinkle with salt. Toss to combine. Cool completely. Serve.

Classic Margherita Pizza

Servings: 4

Ingredients:
- Homemade Pizza Dough:
- 1¾ cups bread flour, plus more for kneading
- ½ teaspoon granulated sugar
- 1⅛ teaspoons instant dry yeast
- 1 teaspoon kosher salt
- ¾ cup warm water (90°–110°F)
- 1 tablespoon plus 1 teaspoon olive oil
- Items Needed:
- Stand mixer with dough hook attachment
- Food processor or blender
- Tomato Sauce:
- 1 can peeled whole San Marzano tomatoes (28-ounces)
- 1½ tablespoons extra virgin olive oil
- ½ teaspoon kosher salt
- ¼ teaspoon dried oregano
- Pizza:
- 1 premade pizza dough
- 1 tablespoon olive oil
- 6 tablespoons tomato sauce
- 1.5 ounces fresh mozzarella
- 8–10 fresh basil leaves, roughly torn

Directions:
1. Homemade Pizza:
2. Combine the flour, sugar, yeast, and salt in the bowl of a stand mixer with the dough hook attached and mix on low speed until well combined.
3. Add the warm water and 1 tablespoon olive oil and beat until the dough forms a ball, about 5 minutes.
4. Scrape the dough onto a lightly floured surface and gently knead into a smooth, firm ball.
5. Grease a large bowl with the remaining 1 teaspoon olive oil.
6. Add the dough, cover the bowl, and allow to rise until doubled in size. This will take about 1 hour, depending on the temperature of your kitchen.
7. Turn the dough out onto a lightly floured surface and divide into 2 equal pieces.
8. Cover each with a clean kitchen towel and let rest for 10 minutes before making your pizza.
9. Classic Margherita Pizza:
10. Drain the tomatoes and reserve the liquid.
11. Place the tomatoes, olive oil, salt, and oregano in a food processor or blender and blend until smooth. Season to taste.
12. Note: Sauce will last 1 week in the refrigerator.Select the Preheat function on the Air Fryer and press Start/Pause.
13. Stretch out the pizza dough into a 7-inch circle on a floured surface.
14. Place the pizza dough into the preheated air fryer. Brush the top with 1 tablespoon olive oil.
15. Set temperature to 400°F and time to 5 minutes, then press Start/Pause.
16. Flip the pizza dough over when the timer goes off and cook at 400°F for an additional 2 minutes.
17. Flip the pizza dough back over when the timer goes off and top with 2 to 3 tablespoons tomato sauce. Use the back of a spoon to spread it evenly across the surface, leaving ½-inch of space around the edge of the crust.
18. Break half of the mozzarella into large pieces and gently place them on top of the sauce.
19. Cook at 400°F for an additional 5 minutes.
20. Remove when the dough is golden brown and the cheese is melted.
21. Top with fresh basil and serve.

Air Fryer Hot Pockets

Servings: 1
Cooking Time: 12 Minutes

Ingredients:
- 1 Frozen Hot Pocket
- EQUIPMENT
- Air Fryer

Directions:
1. Place the frozen hot pocket in the air fryer basket. If cooking multiple hot pockets, spread out into a single even layer. No oil spray is needed.
2. Air Fry at 380°F/193°C for 10 minutes. If needed, flip the hot pocket over and cook for another 1-3 minutes or until cooked to your preference. Cooking more than 1 hot pocket at a time might require more cooking time.

Notes

Air Frying Tips and Notes:
No Oil Necessary. Cook Frozen - Do not thaw first. Shake or turn if needed. Don't overcrowd the air fryer basket.
Recipe timing is based on a non-preheated air fryer. If cooking in multiple batches of hot pockets back to back, the following batches may cook a little quicker.
Recipes were tested in 3.7 to 6 qt. air fryers. If using a larger air fryer, the hot pockets might cook quicker so adjust cooking time.

Air Fryer Totino's Pizza

Servings: 4
Cooking Time: 6 Minutes

Ingredients:

- 1 Totino's Party Pizza

Directions:

1. Remove the frozen pizza from packaging. Lightly spray the air fryer tray or air fryer basket with an air fryer safe cooking spray.
2. Place pizza in basket. No need to preheat air fryer. Air fry at 400 degrees F for 6-8 minutes, until it has a crispy crust and has reached your desired level of crispiness.
3. Serve while hot.

Notes

I love this brand of frozen pizza because they have options for pizza toppings. I love pepperoni, or triple cheese pizza. Unless the pizza is deep dish, the cooking times should be the same.

Air Fryer Sausages

Servings: 8
Cooking Time: 10 Minutes

Ingredients:

- 8 sausages

Directions:

1. Preheat the air fryer to 180C (350F)
2. Pierce each sausage with a knife or fork.
3. Lay sausages in the air fryer basket.
4. Cook for 10 minutes, checking on them and turning them over after 5 minutes.

Notes

Use any sausages you want to - any flavour and any size. For smaller sausages check on them before 10 minutes as they will cook in a quicker time.

3 Cheese Air Fryer Mini Pizzas

Cooking Time: 4 Minutes

Ingredients:

- 1 can biscuits
- ⅓ cup pizza sauce
- ⅓ cup mozzarella cheese shredded
- ⅓ cup cheddar cheese shredded
- 2 tablespoon parmesan cheese grated

Directions:

1. Preheat air fryer to 400°F.
2. Roll out the biscuits into flat circles.
3. Top with the pizza sauce and cheese.
4. Place in the air fryer basket and cook for 4 minutes or until cheese is melted.

Air Fryer Brats

Servings: 6
Cooking Time: 7 Minutes

Ingredients:

- 6 bratwurst uncooked
- 1 serving cooking spray

Directions:

1. Preheat the air fryer to 150C/300F. Spray oil in an air fryer basket.
2. Add the bratwurst in a single layer in the air fryer basket.
3. Cook for 8-10 minutes, flipping halfway through.

Notes

TO STORE: Place leftovers in the refrigerator, covered, for up to 5 days.
TO FREEZE: Place the cooked and cooled brats in a ziplock bag and store it in the freezer for up to two months.
TO REHEAT: Reheat the bratwurst in the microwave, non-stick pan, or air fryer.

SNACKS & APPETIZERS RECIPES

Air Fryer Potato Chips

Servings: 4

Ingredients:
- 4 large Russet Potatoes
- 1 tbsp olive oil
- 1 tsp salt

Directions:
1. Wash the potatoes and pat dry.
2. Use a mandolin slicer or sharp knife and slice the potatoes into 1/8 inch slices.
3. Place the potato slices in a medium bowl of water. Let them soak for at least 30 minutes. The water will get cloudy as they soak.
4. After they have soaked, drain potatoes and rinse them again in cold water and pat dry with a paper towel.
5. Toss the potato slices in the olive oil, and season with salt. Working in batches, place the slices in a single layer in the air fryer basket.
6. Set your oven to Air Frying at 380 degrees F. Cook for 10-15 minutes, depending on the thickness of the cut. Shake the basket halfway through cook time. Cook the chips until they begin to turn golden brown.
7. Remove the chips and place them on a sheet of paper towels until they cool. Garnish with fresh parsley flakes or season with salt to taste.

Air-fryer Healthier Veggie Chips

Servings: 4
Cooking Time: 1 Hr 30 Minutes

Ingredients:
- 1 large washed white potato, cut into 1mm-thick slices
- 300g beetroot, trimmed, cut into 1mm-thick slices
- 150g carrot, trimmed, cut into 1mm-thick slices
- 1 1/2 tbs Woolworths extra virgin olive oil
- 1 sprig rosemary, leaves picked, finely chopped

Directions:
1. Place potato in a medium bowl and cover with cold water. Stand for 15 minutes to soak. Place beetroot and carrot in separate bowls. Add 2 tsp oil to beetroot and carrot bowls and toss to coat.
2. Preheat air fryer to 180°C for 2 minutes. Working in 4 batches, cook beetroot and carrot for 15 minutes, shaking basket every few minutes, or until golden and crisp.
3. Drain potatoes, pat dry with a clean tea towel. Transfer to a dry bowl, add remaining oil and toss to coat. Working in 2 batches, cook potato for 15 minutes, shaking basket every few minutes, or until golden and crisp. Sprinkle chips with rosemary to serve.

Air Fryer Chickpeas Recipe

Servings: 4
Cooking Time: 13 Minutes

Ingredients:
- 1 14 oz Canned chickpeas
- 1 teaspoon smoked paprika or as needed
- 1/2 teaspoon onion powder
- 1/4 teaspoon Cayenne pepper
- 1 Tablespoon Olive oil

Directions:
1. Preheat the oven at 190C/380F for 3 minutes
2. Open the can of chickpeas, drain in a colander and rinse under a cold running water. Make sure the chickpea is drained completely, alternatively dry in with a kitchen towel or paper.
3. In a bowl, combine the drained chickpeas, smoked paprika, onion powder, cayenne pepper, salt, olive oil and mix to combine
4. Pour the seasoned chickpeas in the air fryer basket and spread it out. Cook for 12 to 15 minutes shaking every 5 minutes or so at 190C/390F or until crispy

to your liking. Leave to cool for about 5 minutes and serve. Enjoy!

Notes

Tips

If you like the chickpeas to be soft in the middle then cook it for a lesser time. You can start checking from 10 minutes until the desired texture is achieved.

If time is not of the essence, then you can marinate the chickpeas in the spices for about 10 to 15 minutes before air frying.

While it is tempting to cook the chickpeas at 200C/400F, I would advise against it as it would require shaking more often and might even burn easily too.

Store the chickpea at room temperature

Chickpeas vary in size and that is due to the type of brands you choose, if your legume is on the big side, then you may need to cook it longer than 13 minutes. Start checking from 10 minutes for optimum results.

Do not cook more than 1 can of chickpeas at once in the air fryer to allow for even cooking. Cook in batches if need be.

Air Fryer Ravioli

Servings: 4-6

Ingredients:

- 2 large eggs
- 2 tbsp. whole milk
- 1 c. Italian bread crumbs
- 1/4 c. grated Parmesan, plus more for serving
- 1/4 tsp. kosher salt
- Freshly ground black pepper
- 1 (20-oz.) package refrigerated ravioli
- Cooking spray
- Pesto or marinara, for serving

Directions:

1. In a shallow bowl, whisk eggs and milk. In another shallow bowl, combine bread crumbs and Parmesan; season with salt and a few grinds of pepper.
2. Working one at a time, dip ravioli into egg mixture, then into bread crumb mixture, pressing to adhere. Dip back into egg mixture. Place on a plate.
3. Lightly coat an air-fryer basket with cooking spray. Working in batches, arrange ravioli in basket, spacing about 1/4" apart; spray with cooking spray. Cook at 400°, flipping halfway through and spraying with cooking spray, until golden and cooked through, about 7 minutes.
4. Arrange ravioli on a platter. Top with more Parmesan. Serve warm with pesto alongside for dipping.

Air Fryer Beet Chips

Servings: 4

Cooking Time: 30 Minutes

Ingredients:

- 3 beets
- 1 Tablespoon olive oil
- 1 teaspoon Kosher salt
- 1 teaspoon ground black pepper

Directions:

1. Carefully peel the beets and then slice them to your desired thickness using a mandolin. (Careful, these are sharp!)
2. Add the sliced beets into a medium sized mixing bowl and then coat with olive oil, salt, and pepper. Mix until the beets are coated evenly.
3. Add the beet chips in a single layer into the basket of the air fryer. It's ok to overlap the beet chips slightly.
4. Air fry beet chips at 320 degrees Fahrenheit for 30 minutes, carefully flipping the beef chips halfway through the cooking process.
5. Start checking on the chips with 5 minutes remaining and pull the chips early if they are browning fast. (This will depend on the size and thickness of the slices.)
6. Remove the beet chips for the air fryer basket and place them on a wire cooling rack for a few minutes before serving.

Notes

This recipe was made with a 1700 watt basket style 5.8 quart Cosori air fryer. If you are using a different size or different brand of air fryer, you may need to add a minute or two. All air fryers cook a little differently.

Store any leftover beet chips in an airtight container for up to 3 days.

Consider spicing things up by adding a ¼ teaspoon of cayenne pepper, white pepper, or even some red pepper flakes.

Air Fryer Frozen Tater Tots

Servings: 4

Cooking Time: 14 Minutes

Ingredients:

- 16 ounces tater tots frozen
- seasoning salt to taste

Directions:

1. Preheat air fryer to 400°F.
2. Place tater tots in the air fryer basket in a single layer.
3. Cook for 12-14 minutes shaking the basket halfway through the cooking time.
4. Season with salt to taste and serve.

Notes

Reheat tater tots in the air fryer at the same temperature for only a few minutes.

Air Fryer Potato Skins

Servings: 4

Cooking Time: 11 Minutes

Ingredients:

- 4 medium baked potatoes cooled
- 1 tablespoon oil
- ¼ teaspoon salt or to taste
- 1 cup cheddar cheese
- 2 tablespoons bacon bits
- 1 green onion sliced
- sour cream for serving

Directions:

1. Preheat air fryer to 400°F.
2. Cut baked potatoes in half lengthwise. Use a small spoon to scoop out the flesh, leaving a ¼" shell. Set potato flesh aside for another use.
3. Brush both sides of the potato skins with oil and season with salt.
4. Place potato skins cut side down on the air fryer tray. Air fry for 7-9 minutes or until crisp, flipping halfway.
5. Sprinkle potato skins with cheese and bacon bits. Return to air fryer and cook for an additional 2 minutes or until cheese is melted and bubbly.
6. Top with green onion and serve with sour cream.

Air Fryer Puffed Butter Beans

Servings: 4

Cooking Time: 15 Minutes

Ingredients:

- 1 (16 ounce) can large butter beans, drained and rinsed
- 1 tablespoon olive oil
- 1 teaspoon salt
- 1 teaspoon freshly ground black pepper
- 1 teaspoon garlic powder
- Optional: preferred seasoning blend

Directions:

1. Stir together butter beans, olive oil, salt, pepper, and garlic powder in a bowl until combined. Spread out in the air fryer basket
2. Preheat an air fryer to 400 degrees F (200 degrees C).
3. Air fry until golden and crispy, tossing halfway through, for 12 to 15 minutes.
4. Sprinkle with additional seasonings to taste if you like. Store in an air-tight container for 3 to 5 days.

Crispy Air Fryer Potato Chips

Servings: 4

Cooking Time: 50 Minutes

Ingredients:
- 1 medium russet potato (about 12 ounces)
- 1 tablespoon canola oil
- 1/2 teaspoon kosher salt, plus more for seasoning
- Cooking spray

Directions:
1. Using a mandoline or sharp knife, cut 1 medium russet potato crosswise into very thin slices (about 1/8th-inch thick). Transfer to a large bowl and add enough ice water to cover. Soak for 20 minutes.
2. Drain the potatoes well. Spread them out in a single layer on a double layer of paper towels to dry. Let dry for 10 minutes. Wipe the bowl dry.
3. Heat an air fryer to 370°F. Meanwhile, return the potato slices to the bowl. Add 1 tablespoon canola oil and 1/2 teaspoon kosher salt and toss until evenly combined.
4. Coat the air fryer basket with cooking spray. Add enough potato slices to sit in a single, even layer. Air fry until golden brown and crispy, shaking the basket or rotating the trays or flipping the chips every 4 minutes, 15 to 18 minutes total.
5. Carefully transfer the chips with a slotted spoon or tongs to a serving plate or bowl. Repeat air frying the remaining chips, patting them dry before air frying if needed. Season with more kosher salt while warm.

Recipe Notes
Storage: Air fryer potato chips are best eaten the day they are made. Leftovers can be stored in an airtight container at room temperature and reheated in the air fryer for 2 minutes to re-crisp.

Air Fryer Kale Chips

Servings: 4

Cooking Time: 3 Minutes

Ingredients:
- 1 bunch kale
- 2 teaspoons olive oil
- 1/2 teaspoon salt

Directions:
1. Wash the kale and pat dry until completely dry. Roughly tear the leaves into bite sized pieces.
2. Add the kale to a mixing bowl, then drizzle with olive oil. Using your hands, rub the leaves to ensure they have some oil on them. Sprinkle the salt all over.
3. Transfer the kale to the air fryer basket and air fry at 190C/375F for 3-4 minutes, ensuring they don't burn.
4. Repeat the process until all the kale chips are cooked.

Notes
TO STORE: It's best to store the cooled kale chips in a paper bag at room temperature to prevent them from becoming soggy. They should stay crisp for up to 3 days.

Avocado Fries With Lime Dipping Sauce

Servings: 4

Ingredients:
- 8 ounces 2 small avocados, peeled, pitted and cut into 16 wedges
- 1 large egg (lightly beaten)
- 3/4 cup panko breadcrumbs (I used gluten-free)
- 1 1/4 teaspoons lime chili seasoning salt (such as Tajin Classic)
- For the lime dipping sauce
- 1/4 cup 0% Greek Yogurt
- 3 tablespoons light mayonnaise
- 2 teaspoons fresh lime juice
- 1/2 teaspoon lime chili seasoning salt (such as Tajin Classic)

- 1/8 teaspoon kosher salt

Directions:
1. Air Fryer Directions:
2. Preheat the air-fryer 390F degrees.
3. Place egg in a shallow bowl. On another plate, combine panko with 1 teaspoon Tajin.
4. Season avocado wedges with 1/4 teaspoon Tajin. Dip each piece first in egg, and then in panko.
5. Spray both sides with oil then transfer to the air fryer and cook 7 to 8 minutes turning halfway. Serve hot with dipping sauce.
6. Oven Directions:
7. Preheat the oven 425F, follow directions above and bake on a sheet pan until golden and crisp, 10 to 15 minutes.

Air Fryer Tortilla Chips

Servings: 4
Cooking Time: 6 Minutes

Ingredients:
- 4 corn tortillas small
- 1 tablespoon olive oil
- 1/2 tsp salt

Directions:
1. Using a pastry brush, or oil spray, brush or spray a light coating of oil onto the tortilla triangles.
2. Use a pizza cutter or sharp knife and cut the tortillas into triangles.
3. Place tortilla wedges into the air fryer basket, laying them in a single layer, without overlap.
4. Sprinkle tortilla pieces with salt or other seasonings you may wish to use.
5. Working in batches, air fry at 350 degrees Fahrenheit for 7-9 minutes, turning the chips halfway through cooking time. Chips will be golden brown and crispy when done.

Notes

When air frying, remember that the cook time may vary depending on type of air fryer, and size and type of tortilla pieces. If using larger tortillas, cooking time may need to be adjusted by a couple minutes.

Placing the tortilla slices in a single layer helps them to cook evenly and become crispy.

For additional flavors, you can use additional spices and seasonings. A few bolder flavors you can add would be: curry powder ,white cheddar popcorn powder, or a light sprinkle of chili powder.

You can also add a simple boost of flavor by adding garlic powder, cinnamon, a dash of lime juice and then season with salt before air frying.

Curly Fries In The Air Fryer

Servings: 4
Cooking Time: 10 Minutes

Ingredients:
- 1 package of Arby's Seasoned Curly Fries
- Dipping sauce of your choice

Directions:
1. Preheat your air fryer to 400 degrees.
2. Place a single layer of fries, it is okay if they overlap slightly, into the basket.
3. Cook for 8-10 minutes, shaking the basket halfway through, till the desired crispiness.

Notes

HOW TO REHEAT CURLY FRIES:

Preheat your air fryer.

Add fries to the basket and cook for 3-4 minutes or until hot.

Frozen Waffle Fries In The Air Fryer

Servings: 4
Cooking Time: 8 Minutes

Ingredients:
- 1 pound frozen waffle fries (1/2 bag)
- OPTIONAL
- Dipping sauce of choice

Directions:
1. Preheat your air fryer to 400 degrees F.
2. Place a single layer of frozen waffle fries in your air fryer. They can overlap slightly.

3. Cook the fries for 8 to 10 minutes, carefully shaking the basket halfway through cooking.
4. Remove the waffle fries from the air fryer, serve with your favorite dipping sauce, and enjoy!

Notes

HOW TO REHEAT WAFFLE FRIES IN THE AIR FRYER:

Preheat your air fryer to 350 degrees.

Place your leftover waffle fries in the air fryer and cook for about 2 minutes, until warmed thoroughly.

Air Fryer Baked Sweet Potato

Servings: 2
Cooking Time: 45 Minutes

Ingredients:
- 2 medium sweet potatoes (about 6 ounces)

Directions:
1. Poke hole all over with a fork and place in the air fryer, no foil needed.
2. Air fry 370F 35-45 minutes or until soft.
3. Top with your favorite toppings!

Air-fryer Pineapple Chips

Servings: 4
Cooking Time: 1 Hr

Ingredients:
- 1/2 pineapple, skin removed

Directions:
1. Slice pineapple into 2mm-thick slices. Pat dry with paper towel.
2. Preheat air fryer to 140°C for 2 minutes. Working in 4 batches, place fruit, in a single layer, in basket. Cook for 15 minutes, turning halfway through cooking, or until fruit is dry and crisp. Serve.

Air Fryer French Fries

Servings: 4
Cooking Time: 25 Minutes

Ingredients:
- 2 russet potatoes
- 1 tablespoon extra virgin olive oil
- 1/8 teaspoon salt

Directions:
1. Fill a medium-sized bowl halfway with cold water
2. Peel potatoes (if desired) and cut them into 1/4 inch slices.
3. As you slice the potatoes, add them into the water to soak
4. Drain potatoes and fill bowl back up. Mix the potatoes around like you're rotating a salad with your hands. Drain again. Repeat 5-6 times until water is clear.
5. Dry off potatoes and bowl with a paper towel
6. Add potatoes back to dry bowl. Add extra virgin olive oil and salt. Mix to combine.
7. Cook french fries at 350 degrees for 10 minutes, then at 400 degrees for 15-18 minutes, shaking the basket every 5 minutes.

Air Fryer Zucchini Chips

Servings: 4
Cooking Time: 12 Minutes

Ingredients:
- 1 medium zucchini cut into ½" coins
- 1 beaten egg
- cooking spray
- Crumb Coating
- ⅔ cup Panko bread crumbs
- ⅔ cup seasoned bread crumbs
- 2 tablespoons Parmesan cheese grated
- 1 teaspoon Italian seasoning

Directions:
1. Preheat air fryer to 375°F.
2. Mix coating ingredients in a bowl.

3. Toss zucchini with egg. Dip zucchini into the coating mixture gently pressing to adhere.
4. Lightly spray zucchini with cooking spray.
5. Place in a single layer in the air fryer basket and cook 6 minutes. Turn zucchini over and air fry 6-8 minutes more or until crisp and zucchini is tender.

Notes

For batches, undercook zucchini by 2 minutes. Once all batches are cooked, place them all in the air fryer together for 3 minutes to heat through.Reheat in the air fryer at 375°F for 3-5 minutes or until heated through.

Air Fryer Curly Fries

Servings: 4
Cooking Time: 10 Minutes

Ingredients:
- 16 ounces frozen curly fries
- ½ teaspoon seasoned salt

Directions:
1. Preheat the air fryer to 400°F.
2. Place the frozen fries in the air fryer basket in a single layer.
3. Cook for 9-10 minutes or until golden brown and crispy.
4. Season with salt and serve.

Air Fryer Home Fries

Servings: 4
Cooking Time: 40 Minutes

Ingredients:
- 1 tablespoon olive oil
- 1 ½ pounds russet potatoes
- ½ teaspoon seasoned salt
- ½ teaspoon garlic powder
- ¼ cup onion chopped
- ¼ cup bell pepper red or green, chopped
- 1 tablespoon melted butter

Directions:
1. Peel potatoes (if desired) and cut into ½" chunks.
2. Toss potatoes with olive oil, seasoned salt & garlic powder.
3. Add to the air fryer basket and cook at 380°F for 15 minutes.
4. Combine onion, bell pepper and butter. Add to the air fryer, reduce heat to 340°F and cook an additional 15 minutes or until vegetables and potatoes are tender.
5. Serve immediately.

Notes

Store leftover home fries in the fridge in an airtight container for up to 4 days.

To reheat, put in the microwave for a minute or two or place back in the air fryer for 5 minutes or until heated through.

Blistered Snap Peas

Servings: 4

Ingredients:
- 1 lb. snap peas, strings removed
- 2 tbsp. olive oil
- 1/2 to 1 teaspoon gochugaru
- Kosher salt
- 1/2 lemon, plus wedges for serving
- Cilantro, for serving

Directions:
1. Place grill basket on grill and heat grill and basket, covered, on high 10 minutes.
2. In large bowl, toss snap peas with oil, gochugaru, and 1/2 teaspoon salt. Add to grill basket and grill, tossing twice, until charred and just tender, 5 to 8 minutes.
3. Squeeze juice of 1/2 lemon on top and toss to combine. Transfer to shallow bowl or platter and serve with additional wedges and sprinkle with cilantro if desired.
4. AIR FRYER DIRECTIONS:
5. Heat air fryer to 400°F. In large bowl, toss snap peas with oil, gochugaru and 1/2 teaspoon salt. Add snap peas to air-fryer basket and air-fry until slightly charred and just tender, 5 to 6 minutes.

Squeeze juice of lemon half on top. Using tongs, quickly toss to combine, then transfer snap peas to shallow bowl or platter. Serve with lemon wedges and sprinkle with cilantro.

Roasted Garlic Green Beans

Servings: 4

Cooking Time: 10 Minutes

Ingredients:

- 1 lb. green beans, washed and trimmed
- 1 tablespoon garlic, minced
- 1 tablespoon vegetable oil
- 1 teaspoon sesame oil
- 1 teaspoon Italian seasoning
- 1 teaspoon Worcestershire sauce
- 1 teaspoon balsamic vinegar
- 1 teaspoon soy sauce
- 1/2 teaspoon black pepper (or to taste)

Directions:

1. Preheat oven to 375 F (or preheat air fryer to 350 F).
2. Wash and trim the green beans, then dry them with a paper towel. Place them into a large mixing bowl and add all remaining ingredients. Toss to combine.
3. Roast in the oven: Transfer the green beans onto a quarter sheet baking pan and spread them out evenly. Bake for 15 minutes until tender, but still crunchy.
4. Cook in the air fryer: Transfer the green beans into the air fryer basket and cook at 350 F for 10 minutes until tender, but still crunchy. Shake the basket halfway through cooking.

Notes

How to store: Store green beans in an airtight container for up to 4 days in the refrigerator. Reheat in a 300F preheated oven or air fryer for 5-10 minutes, until warmed through.

How to use the sauce: The balance of tangy, sour, savoury and sweet flavours in the sauce make it an excellent choice to use for any roasted vegetable such as brussels sprouts, potatoes, butternut squash and more.

How to add toppings: These green beans are delicious just the way they are. You could also add some toppings if you please. Some great options are crushed peanuts or pecans, and crispy bacon.

Air Fryer Spicy Onion Rings

Servings: 4

Cooking Time: 10 Minutes

Ingredients:

- 2 large sweet onions, sliced 1/2 inch thick
- Batter:
- ⅔ cup buttermilk
- 1 egg
- ¼ cup all-purpose flour
- 1 teaspoon RedHot Chile and Lime Seasoning Blend (such as Frank's®)
- ½ teaspoon adobo all-purpose seasoning (such as Goya®)
- Breading:
- 2 cups panko bread crumbs
- 1 teaspoon adobo all-purpose seasoning (such as Goya®)
- ½ teaspoon RedHot Chile and Lime Seasoning Blend (such as Frank's®)
- olive oil cooking spray
- 1 teaspoon kosher salt, or to taste

Directions:

1. Whisk together buttermilk, egg, flour, chile and lime seasoning, and adobo seasoning for the batter in a shallow bowl. Cover and refrigerate for 30 minutes.
2. Combine panko, adobo seasoning, and chile and lime seasoning in a shallow dish; mix well. Remove batter from the fridge. Dip onion rings first into the batter, then into bread crumb mixture, turning to coat, and gently shake off excess crumbs. Lightly spritz the onion rings with cooking spray on both sides.

3. Preheat the air fryer to 340 degrees F (170 degrees C). Line the air fryer basket with a parchment liner or lightly spray with oil.
4. Place the breaded onion rings into the fryer basket in an even layer, leaving about 1/2-inch space between the slices.
5. Cook until crisp and lightly browned, flipping halfway through, 10 to 12 minutes. You may have to cook in batches, and cooking time may vary depending on the size and brand of your air fryer.
6. Remove from the air fryer, transfer to a baking sheet, sprinkle with kosher salt, and place in a 250 degrees F (120 degrees C) oven to keep warm.
7. Cook's Notes:
8. You can find Chile n' Lime seasoning and Adobo seasoning in the Hispanic section of your supermarket. Adobo should be available at most stores, but if Chile n' Lime is not, use all Adobo.
9. Chilling the batter will make the breading adhere better. You may bread the onion rings, cover early in the day, and refrigerate until ready to cook.

SANDWICHES & BURGERS RECIPES

Keto Friendly Game Day Burgers

Ingredients:
- Mini Beef Burgers:
- 1.5 pounds ground beef
- 1/4 cup onion, diced
- 1 tsp salt
- 1/4 tsp pepper
- 1 tsp brown Mustard
- Low Carb Sauce:
- 1/2 cup mayonnaise
- 1 tsp white wine vinegar
- 1 tsp paprika
- 1 tsp garlic powder
- 1 tsp onion powder
- 4 tbsp dill pickle relish

Directions:
1. Using your hands mix together the beef, onion, salt, pepper, and brown sugar (optional.)
2. Form into 15-20 mini balls.
3. Cook in your air fryer, flipping half way to your desired doneness, 7-8 minutes at 390 degrees.
4. While the burgers are cooking, mix your mayonnaise, white vinegar, paprika, garlic powder, onion powder, and dill pickle relish together. Set to the side.
5. Place each burger on a skewer with cheese, lettuce, pickles, and the special sauce.
6. Enjoy!

Air Fryer Hamburgers

Servings: 4
Cooking Time: 8 Minutes

Ingredients:
- 1-pound ground beef, thawed (preferably 80/20)
- 1 clove garlic, minced
- 1/2 teaspoon salt
- 1/4 teaspoon pepper

Directions:
1. Preheat air fryer to 360 degrees.
2. Mix together the ground beef, minced garlic, salt, and pepper with your hands.
3. Form ground beef into 4 patties and press them down with the back of a pie plate to make them evenly flat.
4. Place hamburgers in a single layer inside the air fryer.
5. Cook for 8-12 minutes, flipping halfway through cooking for medium-well hamburgers.*
6. Carefully remove hamburgers from the air fryer,** place onto hamburger buns (if using), and add desired toppings.

Notes

thicker hamburgers may take longer to cook if not pressed down properly

if making cheeseburgers, place a piece of cheese on each burger in the air fryer, turn the air fryer off, and let the burgers sit in the air fryer for 1 to 2 minutes until melted

Air Fried Crispy Chicken Sandwiches

Servings: 4

Ingredients:
- 2 large chicken breasts, cut in half and pounded to an even thickness
- 1 cup buttermilk
- 1 tablespoon kosher salt or 1 teaspoon table salt
- ¾ cup panko breadcrumbs
- ½ cup all-purpose flour
- ½ teaspoon salt
- ¼ teaspoon dried oregano
- ½ teaspoon paprika
- ¼ teaspoon garlic powder
- ¼ teaspoon dried thyme
- ¼ teaspoon ground ginger

- ½ teaspoon ground black pepper
- Oil spray
- 4 brioche burger buns
- Assorted toppings such as lettuce, tomato, onions and additional condiments

Directions:
1. Place the chicken breasts in a zipper top bag and pour in buttermilk and salt. Squeeze the air out and seal the bag. Marinate in the refrigerator for at least an hour or preferably overnight.
2. In a shallow bowl combine the panko breadcrumbs, flour and spices.
3. Remove the chicken breasts from the buttermilk. Remove excess buttermilk and dredge in the breadcrumb mixture.
4. Arrange the chicken breasts in one layer on a parchment-lined baking sheet, thoroughly coating chicken with oil spray on both sides.
5. Air Fry at 375°F for 20 – 25 minutes or until internal temperature reads 165°F and the chicken breasts are golden brown and crispy. For more even cooking, flip the chicken halfway through and spray with more oil if desired.
6. Serve chicken sandwiches on toasted brioche buns with lettuce, tomatoes, red onion and other favorite condiments.

Air Fryer Grilled Cheese Sandwich

Servings: 2
Cooking Time: 7 Minutes

Ingredients:
- 8 slices white bread
- 1 tablespoon butter
- 4 slices cheese

Directions:
1. Spread a light layer of the butter on one side of each piece of bread.
2. Place the buttered side down in the air fryer basket.
3. Cover the slice of bread with a piece of cheese. Then top the cheese with another slice of bread, with the buttered side up.
4. Air Fry at 370 degrees F for 3-5 minutes. Then flip, and air fry for 2-3 additional minutes, until bread reaches desired crispness.

Notes
Make this a heartier meal by adding a few slices of bacon to the sandwich, avocado slices, or on inside of slices, spread bread with pesto sauce before adding cheese.
Depending on the type of bread you use, you may want to adjust the cook times. For softer bread, or French Bread, air fry until it reaches your desired crispness.

Air Fryer Bacon, Egg And Cheese Biscuit Breakfast Sandwiches

Servings: 8

Ingredients:
- 1 can (16.3 oz) refrigerated Pillsbury™ Grands!™ Southern Homestyle Original Biscuits (8 Count)
- 6 eggs
- 1/4 teaspoon salt
- 1/8 teaspoon pepper, if desired
- 1 tablespoon butter
- 8 slices cooked bacon, cut in half crosswise
- 8 slices (3/4 oz each) American cheese

Directions:
1. Spray bottom of air fryer basket with cooking spray. Separate dough into 8 biscuits. Place 4 biscuits in air fryer basket, spacing apart.
2. Set air fryer to 330°F; cook 6 minutes. Using tongs or spatula, turn over each biscuit. Cook 4 to 5 minutes or until biscuits are deep golden brown and cooked through. Remove from air fryer; cover loosely with foil to keep warm while cooking second batch. Cook remaining biscuits as directed above.
3. Meanwhile, in medium bowl, beat eggs, salt and pepper thoroughly with fork or whisk until well mixed. In 10-inch skillet, heat butter over medium heat just until butter begins to sizzle. Pour egg mixture into skillet. Cook until set, stirring occasionally.

4. To serve, split warm biscuits; top bottom half of each with scrambled eggs, bacon and cheese. Cover with top halves of biscuits.

Air Fryer Frozen Burger

Servings: 2
Cooking Time: 15 Minutes

Ingredients:
- 2 frozen burger patties

Directions:
1. Place frozen burgers in a single layer in the basket of the air fryer.
2. Air fry the burgers at 350 degrees Fahrenheit for 15 minutes, flipping the burgers halfway through cook time.
3. If desired, add sliced cheese during the last minute of cooking time.
4. Carefully remove the burgers from the air fryer and serve them with your favorite toppings.

Notes
If adding cheese, top with sliced cheese during the last minute of cook time.
Serve bunless for a healthier burger.

Air Fryer Chicken Burgers

Servings: 4
Cooking Time: 10 Minutes

Ingredients:
- 1 pound ground chicken
- 1 large egg
- 1 cup mozzarella cheese shredded
- 1/2 cup onion finely chopped
- 1/2 cup panko breadcrumbs
- 1 teaspoon minced garlic
- 1/2 teaspoon kosher salt
- 1/4 teaspoon ground black pepper

Directions:
1. Preheat air fryer to 365 degrees F.
2. In a large bowl, combine the chicken, egg, cheese, onion, panko crumbs, garlic, salt and pepper. Mix chicken mixture together with your hands until fully combined.
3. Divide the chicken mixture into 4 equal parts and shape them into 5-inch diameter burgers.
4. Spray the air fryer basket with non-stick cooking spray and place the chicken patties in air fryer in a single layer.
5. Air fry the chicken burgers at 365 degrees F for 8-10 minutes or until cooked through, depending on the thickness of the patties.
6. Use a meat thermometer to confirm internal temperature of burger patties which should be a safe temperature of 165 degrees F.
7. Allow chicken burgers to cool for a couple of minutes then carefully remove them from the basket.
8. Serve while hot or let them continue to rest on a baking rack.

Notes
Optional Additional Favorite Sauces: BBQ sauce, mustard yogurt sauce, chili sauce, ketchup, spicy sriracha sauce (based on your spice level), honey mustard, marinara sauce, relish or a sweet and spicy pickle.
Optional Favorite Toppings: Shredded lettuce, slice of tomato, raw or caramelized onions, sundried tomato strips, bacon, avocado, pepper jack cheese, American cheese or shredded cheese.
Cooking Tips: Use a silicone mat to make it an easy clean up and prevent food sticking to your basket. For crispy chicken patties brush a little olive oil on the patties prior to placing them in your air fryer.
I make this recipe in my Cosori 5.8 qt. air fryer. Depending on your air fryer, size and wattages, your cooking time may need to be adjusted 1-2 minutes.

Greek Lamb Burgers With Baked Eggplant Fries

Servings: 4

Ingredients:
- Nonstick cooking spray
- 1 pound ground lamb
- 2 ounces feta cheese, crumbled (about ½ cup)
- ½ cup grated red onion (from 1 small onion), divided
- 1 ½ tablespoon olive oil, divided
- 2 ½ teaspoons kosher salt, divided
- ¾ teaspoon freshly ground black pepper, divided
- 1 ½ cups panko
- 2 large egg whites
- 1 medium eggplant, cut into ½-by-1-by-2-in. wedges
- ½ cup grated English cucumber (from ½ cucumber)
- 1 cup plain whole-milk Greek yogurt
- 2 teaspoons fresh lemon juice (from 1 lemon)
- Hamburger buns and lettuce, for serving

Directions:
1. Preheat oven to 425°F. Lightly coat a rimmed baking sheet with cooking spray. Stir together lamb, cheese, ¼ cup onion, 1 tablespoon oil, 1 teaspoon salt, and ½ teaspoon pepper in a bowl until just combined; shape into 4 patties.
2. Combine panko and remaining 1½ teaspoons salt in a large ziplock plastic bag. Whisk egg whites in a large bowl until foamy. Dip eggplant wedges, 1 at a time, in egg whites and transfer to bag with panko. Once all eggplant has been added to bag, seal and shake well to coat. Arrange eggplant in an even layer on prepared baking sheet and coat generously with cooking spray. Bake until golden brown, about 20 minutes, flipping halfway through.
3. Meanwhile, heat remaining ½ tablespoon oil in a large nonstick skillet over medium-high. Add lamb patties and cook, flipping once, until browned, about 4 minutes per side for medium.
4. Place cucumber and remaining ¼ cup onion on a paper towel. Squeeze gently to release liquid. Transfer to a small bowl and stir in yogurt, lemon juice, and remaining ¼ teaspoon pepper.
5. Place patties on buns with lettuce and yogurt sauce. Serve with eggplant fries and remaining yogurt sauce.

Air Fryer Biscuit Egg Sandwiches

Servings: 4

Ingredients:
- Deselect All
- Nonstick cooking spray, for the molds
- 4 large eggs
- Kosher salt
- 4 thin slices deli ham
- One 16.3-ounce tube refrigerated flaky biscuit dough, such as Pillsbury
- Hot sauce, for serving

Directions:
1. Special equipment: 4 silicone baking cups, 6-quart air fryer
2. Spray 4 silicone baking cups with nonstick spray. Transfer the cups to the basket of a 6-quart air fryer.
3. Whisk together the eggs in a large glass measuring cup until no white streaks remain. Season with 1/2 teaspoon salt. Divide the eggs among the baking cups. Insert a piece of ham into each cup, crumpling it to make it fit (some of the ham should stick out above the surface of the eggs).
4. Tear off 4 biscuits from the tube of dough. Place each biscuit in the basket of the air fryer in a single layer. Set the air fryer to 300 degrees F and cook for 10 minutes. The biscuits should be golden brown; transfer to a cutting board.
5. Gently lift each egg muffin from its mold so you can see if it's set. If there's no liquid egg on the bottom, transfer the mold to the cutting board. If there is liquid egg on the bottom, cook for up to 1 minute more.

6. Slice each biscuit in half crosswise. Remove the egg muffins from the molds and slice in half crosswise. Arrange the two egg halves on each bottom biscuit, drizzle with plenty of hot sauce and sandwich with the top biscuit.

Air Fryer Burgers From Frozen Patties

Servings: 4
Cooking Time: 15 Minutes

Ingredients:
- 4 frozen raw beef patties , usually sold as either 1/4 lb.(113g) or 1/3 lb.(150g)
- salt , to taste if needed
- Lots of black pepper
- oil spray , for coating
- BURGER ASSEMBLY:
- 4 Buns , + optional cheese, pickles, lettuce, onion, tomato, avocado, cooked bacon etc.
- EQUIPMENT
- Air Fryer
- Instant Read Thermometer (optional)

Directions:

1. Spray both sides of frozen burger patties with oil. Season with salt and pepper if needed. Spray the air fryer basket with oil and place the patties in the basket in a single layer. Cook in batches if needed.
2. For 1/4 lb. frozen burger patties: Air Fry at 360°F/180°C for a total of about 8-12 minutes. After the first 6 minutes flip the patties and continue to Air Frying at 360°F/180°C for another 2-6 minutes or until it's cooked to your preferred doneness. The internal temperature should be 160°F/71°C.
3. For 1/3 lb. frozen burger patties: Air Fry at 360°F/180°C for a total of about 12-16 minutes. After the first 10 minutes flip the patties and continue to Air Frying at 360°F/180°C for another 2-6 minutes or until it's cooked to your preferred doneness. The internal temperature should be 160°F/71°C.
4. For Cheeseburgers: add the slices of cheese on top of the cooked patties. Air fry at 360°F/180°C for about 30 seconds to 1 minute to melt the cheese.
5. Cover the patties and let rest for 3 minutes. Warm the buns in the air fryer at 380°F/193°C for about 3 minutes while patties are resting. Serve on buns, topped with your favorite burger toppings.

FISH & SEAFOOD RECIPES

Air Fryer Oven Cheesy Scalloped Potatoes

Ingredients:
- 3 tablespoons butter
- 1 small white or yellow onion, peeled and thinly sliced
- 4 large garlic cloves, minced
- 1/4 cup all-purpose flour
- 1 cup chicken stock or vegetable stock
- 2 cups milk (2% or whole milk, recommended)
- 1 1/2 teaspoons Kosher salt
- 1/2 teaspoon black pepper
- 2 teaspoons fresh thyme leaves, divided
- 10 Yukon Gold Potatoes, sliced into 1/8-inch rounds
- 2 cups freshly-grated sharp cheddar cheese*, divided
- 1/2 cup freshly-grated Parmesan cheese, plus extra for serving

Directions:
1. Prep oven and baking dish: Pre-heat air fryer to 400°F. Grease a 8 x 8-inch baking dish with cooking spray, and set it aside.
2. Sauté the onion and garlic. Melt butter in a large sauté pan over medium-high heat. Add onion, and sauté for 4-5 minutes until soft and translucent. Add garlic and sauté for an additional 1-2 minutes until fragrant. Stir in the flour until it is evenly combined, and cook for 1 more minute.
3. Simmer the sauce. Gradually pour in the stock, and whisk until combined. Add in the milk, salt, pepper, and 1 teaspoon thyme, and whisk until combined. Continue cooking for an additional 1-2 minutes until the sauce just barely begins to simmer around the edges of the pan and thickens. Then remove from heat and set aside.
4. Layer the potatoes. Spread half of the sliced potatoes in an even layer on the bottom of the pan. Top evenly with half of the cream sauce. Then sprinkle evenly with 1 cup of the shredded cheddar cheese, and all of the Parmesan cheese. Top evenly with the remaining sliced potatoes, the other half of the cream sauce, and the remaining 1 cup of cheddar cheese.
5. Bake: Cover the pan with aluminum foil and bake at 400 degrees for 40 minutes. The sauce should be nice and bubbly around the edges. Then remove the foil and bake uncovered for 10-15 minutes, or until the potatoes are cooked through.
6. Cool. Transfer the pan to a cooling rack, and sprinkle with the remaining teaspoon of thyme and extra Parmesan.
7. Serve. Serve warm.

Air Fryer Shrimp

Servings: 4
Cooking Time: 7 Minutes

Ingredients:
- 1 lb shrimp large or extra large
- 1 tablespoon olive oil
- 1/2 tablespoon lemon juice
- 1/2 teaspoon salt
- 1/2 teaspoon pepper
- 1/2 teaspoon garlic
- 1/2 teaspoon smoked paprika
- 1 teaspoon Italian seasonings

Directions:
1. Pat dry shrimp with a paper towel.
2. In a mixing bowl, whisk together the olive oil and lemon juice. Add the seasonings and mix well. Toss through the shrimp in the seasoning mix.
3. Cook the shrimp at 200C/400F for 7-8 minutes.
4. Serve immediately.

Notes

TO STORE: Air fryer shrimp can be stored in the refrigerator for up to 3 days in an air-tight container.

TO FREEZE: Place leftovers in a ziplock bag and store it in the freezer for up to 2 months.

TO REHEAT: Thaw and then put on the baking sheet or in the air fryer basket to reheat until crispy.

Air Fryer Scallops

Servings: 4

Cooking Time: 5 Minutes

Ingredients:

- 1/2 lb scallops
- 1/2 teaspoon salt
- 1/4 teaspoon pepper
- 2 tablespoons butter divided
- 1/4 cup parsley finely chopped
- 1/2 small lemon sliced

Directions:

1. Pat dry the scallops and then sprinkle with salt and pepper. Brush one tablespoon of butter over the scallops.
2. Generously grease an air fryer basket with cooking spray and add a single layer of scallops.
3. Air fry at 200C/400 for 5-7 minutes, flipping halfway through.
4. Remove them from the air fryer basket, and brush more butter on them. Sprinkle with finely chopped parsley and serve with sliced lemon.

Notes

TO STORE: Place leftover scallops in a shallow container and store them in the refrigerator for up to two days.

TO FREEZE: Once the scallops have cooled to room temperature, place them in a shallow container and store them in the freezer for up to two months.

TO REHEAT: Reheat in the air fryer or microwave until warm.

Air Fryer Salmon And Swiss Chard

Servings: 4

Ingredients:

- 1 medium red onion (sliced 1/2 inch thick)
- 1 1/2 tbsp. oil, divided
- Kosher salt and pepper
- 1 large bunch red Swiss chard (thick stems discarded, leaves chopped)
- 2 cloves garlic (sliced)
- 4 5-oz. salmon fillets
- Chili oil, for serving

Directions:

1. Heat air fryer to 385°F. Toss onion with 1/2 tablespoon oil and a pinch each of salt and pepper and air-fry 5 minutes.
2. Toss with Swiss chard, garlic, 1 tablespoon oil, and 1/4 teaspoon each salt and pepper and air-fry until chard and onion are just tender, about 5 minutes more. Transfer to plates.
3. Season salmon with 1/2 teaspoon each salt and pepper and air-fry at 400°F until skin is crispy and salmon is opaque throughout, 8 to 10 minutes. Serve with chard and drizzle with chili oil if desired.

Air Fryer Keto Coconut Shrimp

Servings: 8

Cooking Time: 10 Minutes

Ingredients:

- 25 large shrimp peeled and deveined
- 1/2 cup coconut flour
- 1 3/4 cup coconut flakes unsweetened
- 3 eggs
- 1 tbsp ground black pepper
- 1 tsp smoked paprika
- 1 tsp salt

Directions:

1. Preheat the Air Fryer to 390 degrees Fahrenheit. Prepare the air fryer basket with non stick cooking spray.

2. Arrange three bowls. Add the coconut flour, paprika, salt and pepper to one bowl. Coconut flakes to the second bowl, and beaten eggs in the third bowl.
3. Dip the shrimp into the coconut flour mixture, then dip into the egg mixture, and finally into the coconut flakes. Set aside on a wire rack until you've finished with all of the shrimp.
4. Add the coconut shrimp in a single layer into the prepared air fryer basket and cook for 8-10 minutes at 380 degrees Fahrenheit. Flip the shrimp halfway through.
5. Remove when golden brown and serve immediately.

Notes

If you have any "hanging" coconut flakes they will likely brown faster than the shrimp. Air fryers also cook differently and have different wattages. You may need to add or take away time for this recipe depending on the type of air fryer you own.

Air Fryer Bacon Wrapped Scallops

Servings: 4
Cooking Time: 13 Minutes

Ingredients:

- 16 large sea scallops cleaned & pat dry with paper towels
- 8 slices center cut bacon
- 1/4 cup Williamson Bros. BBQ sauce

Directions:

1. Slice bacon in half and place the bacon in the air fryer to partially cook at 400 for 3 minutes.
2. 16 large sea scallops
3. Pat the scallops dry with paper towels to remove any moisture.
4. Wrap each scallop in 1/2 slice of bacon and secure it with a toothpick.
5. 8 slices center cut bacon
6. Place scallops in air fryer (I can fit 8 at a time in my basket style air fryer)
7. Lightly brush scallop with your favorite barbecue sauce. I recommend a thinner sauce – not a heavy thick sauce. You can also just spray with olive oil and salt/pepper.
8. Cook at 400 for 5 minutes. Turn scallops delicately and baste again with bbq sauce. Cook for another 5 minutes at 400 until scallop is tender and opaque and bacon is cooked through. Serve hot.
9. 1/4 cup Williamson Bros. BBQ sauce
10. I also sprinkled a little Historic BBQ Red seasoning on them when they were done.

Air Fryer Blackened Mahi Mahi

Servings: 4
Cooking Time: 9 Minutes

Ingredients:

- 4 mahi mahi fillets 3-4 oz each
- 2 tablespoons olive oil
- 3 tablespoons blackening seasoning

Directions:

1. Preheat air fryer to 400°F.
2. Pat fillets dry and generously rub with olive oil then coat them with blackening seasoning.
3. Place fillets in the air fryer basket and cook for 7-9 minutes.
4. Fish should reach 145°F internally and be opaque and flaky.

Notes

For the best crispy crust, preheat the air fryer first. If cooking in batches, keep warm in the oven and broil before serving.

Cooking time can vary with the thickness of the fish. Check the temperature of the fish early to ensure it doesn't overcook.

Serving Suggestion: Serve with fruit salsa like pineapple salsa or the quick bell pepper salsa below.

Quick Bell Pepper Salsa (optional): Dice one Roma tomato, half a bell pepper, and two tablespoons of red onion. Season with a squeeze of lime juice, a teaspoon of olive oil, and salt and pepper. Add a sprinkle of cilantro.

Fish 'n' Chips

Servings: 4

Ingredients:
- For the chips
- 700g King Edward or Maris Piper potatoes
- 2 tbsp sunflower oil
- Sea salt
- 2 tsp semolina (optional)
- lemon wedges and parsley to garnish
- For the fish
- 2 slices stale bread, crusts removed and torn into pieces
- 1 garlic clove
- 1 zest of lemon
- 5g fresh parsley, leaves and stalks
- sea salt and pepper to taste
- 1 x 120g chunky thick skinless cod fillets, pat dry
- 2 tbsp oil
- COOKING MODE
- When entering cooking mode - We will enable your screen to stay 'always on' to avoid any unnecessary interruptions whilst you cook!

Directions:
1. Peel potatoes and cut into 5cm thick chips. Place in a bowl, cover with water and allow to soak for 30 minutes to remove excess starch. Rinse and pat potatoes dry.
2. In a clean bowl, add chips, oil, salt and semolina. Toss together to make sure the chips are coated. Insert crisper plates into both drawers and add the chips to Zone 1 drawer.
3. Place bread, garlic, lemon, parsley and seasoning into a food processor. Whizz until you have fine breadcrumbs. Add oil and pulse until mixed. Spoon breadcrumb topping onto cod. Press topping on with the back of spoon. Spray Zone 2 drawer and carefully place topped cod into drawer.
4. Select Zone 1, turn the dial to select AIR FRY, set temperature to 200°C, and set time to 26 minutes. Select Zone 2 and turn the dial to select ROAST, set temperature to 170°C and set time to 14 minutes. Select SYNC. Press the dial to begin cooking.
5. After 10 minutes, shake Zone 1 drawer, shake again after 15 and 20 minutes. Check at 24 minutes if cooked enough.
6. When cooking time is complete, remove fish and chips and serve with tartar sauce and mushy peas.

Air-fried Beer Battered Fish Tacos With Mango Salsa Recipe

Ingredients:
- For the fish:
- 2 eggs
- 10 ounces of Mexican beer
- 1 1/2 cups of corn starch
- 1 1/2 cups of flour
- 1/2 tablespoon of chili powder
- 1 tablespoon of cumin
- Kosher salt and fresh cracked pepper to taste
- 1 pound of cod cut into large pieces
- Non-stick spray
- For the Salsa & to make the Taco:
- 3 peeled and medium-diced mangos
- 1/2 peeled, seeded and small diced red bell pepper
- 1 peeled, seeded and small diced jalapeno
- 1/2 peeled and small diced red onion
- 1 tablespoon of chopped fresh cilantro
- Juice of 1 lime
- Kosher salt and fresh cracked pepper to taste
- 1/2thinly sliced head of red cabbage
- Soft corn tortillas
- Crumbled queso fresco for garnish
- Sliced green onions and cilantro leaves for garnish

Directions:
1. For the salsa:
2. Combine the mangos, peppers, onion, chopped cilantro, lime juice together in a medium size bowl and mix. Refrigerate until ready to serve.
3. For the fish:

4. In a medium size bowl whisk together the eggs and beer and set aside.
5. In a separate medium bowl whisk together the cornstarch, flour, chili powder, cumin, salt and pepper.
6. Coat the fish in the egg-beer mixture and transfer it to the flour mixture and dredge to completely coat on all sides.
7. Spray the bottom of the air fryer basket with no-stick spray and place in the fish and spray the tops of the fish with no-stick spray.
8. Cook at 375 degrees for 15 minutes
9. Place the air fried fish on a corn tortilla and top off with cabbage, salsa, queso fresco, green onions, and cilantro.
10. Enjoy!

Frozen Shrimp In The Air Fryer

Servings: 4
Cooking Time: 7 Minutes

Ingredients:

- 1 pound frozen cooked large shrimp
- 1 tablespoon unsalted butter, melted
- 1 tablespoon Old Bay seasoning
- ½ tablespoon lemon juice
- 1 teaspoon minced garlic

Directions:

1. Heat air fryer to 350 degrees F.
2. Break apart frozen shrimp and place the shrimp, butter, Old Bay seasoning, lemon juice, and garlic in a large bowl. Stir to combine and coat all of the shrimp.
3. In a single layer lay your shrimp (about ½ a pound per batch) and cook for 6 to 7 minutes until fully heated.

Air Fryer Salmon With Maple Soy Glaze

Servings: 4
Cooking Time: 8 Minutes

Ingredients:

- 3 tbsp pure maple syrup
- 3 tbsp reduced sodium soy sauce (or gluten-free soy sauce)
- 1 tbsp sriracha hot sauce
- 1 clove garlic (smashed)
- 4 wild salmon fillets (skinless (6 oz each))

Directions:

1. Combine maple syrup, soy sauce, sriracha and garlic in a small bowl, pour into a gallon sized resealable bag and add the salmon.
2. Marinate 20 to 30 minutes, turning once in a while.
3. Lightly spray the basket with oil.
4. Remove the fish from the marinade, reserving and pat dry with paper towels.
5. Place the fish in the air fryer, in batches, air fry 400F 7 to 8 minutes, or longer depending on thickness of the salmon.
6. Meanwhile, pour the marinade in a small saucepan and bring to a simmer over medium-low heat and reduce until it thickens into a glaze, 1 to 2 minutes. Spoon over salmon just before eating.

Air Fryer Crispy Fish Fillets

Servings: 3
Cooking Time: 15 Minutes

Ingredients:

- 1 pound (454 g) white fish fillets (cod, halibut, tilapia, etc.)
- 1 teaspoon (5 ml) kosher salt , or to taste
- 1/2 teaspoon (2.5 ml) black pepper , or to taste
- 1 teaspoon (5 ml) garlic powder
- 1 teaspoon (5 ml) paprika
- 1-2 cups (60-120 g) breading of choice breadcrumbs, panko, crushed pork rinds or almond flour

- 1 egg, or more if needed
- Cooking Spray
- EQUIPMENT
- Air Fryer
- Air Fryer Parchment Paper (optional)
- Perforated Silicone Mats (optional)

Directions:

1. Preheat the Air Fryer at 380°F/193°C for 4 minutes.
2. If using frozen filets, make sure to thaw first. Cut fish filets in half if needed. Make sure they are even sized so they'll cook evenly. The thicker they are, the longer they will take to cook. Pat the filets dry. Lightly oil the filets and then season with the salt, black pepper, garlic powder, and paprika.
3. Put the breading in a shallow bowl. In another bowl, beat the eggs. Dip the filets in the egg, shaking off excess egg. Dredge the filets in your breading of choice. Press filets into the bowl of breading so that they completely coat the filets. Repeat this process for all fish pieces.
4. Line air fryer basket or tray with perforated parchment paper or perforated silicone mat (highly recommended - if you don't have perforated parchment paper or mat, make sure to generously coat the air fryer basket with oil spray). Lightly spray parchment paper with oil spray. Lay coated fish in a single layer on the parchment (cook in batches if needed). Generously spray all sides of the breaded filets with oil spray to coat any dry spots.
5. Air Fry at 380°F/193°C for 8-14 minutes, depending on the size and thickness of your filets. After 6 minutes, flip the filets. Lightly spray any dry spots than then continue cooking for the remaining time or until they are crispy brown and the fish is cooked through. Serve with your favorite dip: tartar sauce, mustard, aioli, etc.

Cajun Air Fryer Fish

Ingredients:

- Fresh fish fillets. Use any sustainable white fish. I used hake but halibut, cod, tilapia, bass, grouper, haddock, snapper or catfish will all work well.
- Olive oil - Vegetable oil like avocado oil is a good substitution
- Cajun seasoning/Cajun spice. Most supermarkets will have a cajun spice blend in their spice aisle.
- Smoked paprika
- Garlic powder. Onion powder can also be used
- Fresh lemon juice

Directions:

1. Slice the fish into portions then place in the air fryer basket. In a small bowl, mix the olive oil, lemon juice and seasonings together then spoon over the fish. I don't usually add parchment paper to the basket but you can if you're worried about the fish sticking. You can also spray the basket with cooking spray or olive oil. Air fry for 8-10 minutes at 200°C/400°F until the fish is caramelized on the outside and opaque and juicy on the inside. Cooking time will depend on the thickness of the fish but generally fish is cooked when it flakes apart easily and a fork can be inserted without any resistance. Remove from the air fryer then serve with lemon wedges.

Air Fryer Salmon In 6 Minutes Tender And Flaky

Servings: 4
Cooking Time: 6 Minutes

Ingredients:

- 4 fillets salmon 6 oz each
- 1 tablespoon olive oil
- 1/2 teaspoon salt
- 1/2 teaspoon pepper
- 2 tablespoons brown sugar
- 1/2 teaspoon smoked paprika
- 1/2 teaspoon garlic powder

- 1/2 teaspoon onion powder

Directions:
1. In a small bowl, coat the salmon with oil, then add the salt and pepper.
2. Mix the remaining sugar and spices and rub over the salmon.
3. Add the salmon skin side down to the air fryer basket and air fry at 200C/400F for 6 minutes, or until cooked.
4. Remove from the air fryer basket and sprinkle with chopped parsley.

Notes
TO STORE: Leftovers can be stored in an air-tight container in the refrigerator for up to 3 days.
TO FREEZE: Place the cooked and cooled salmon in a ziplock bag and store it in the freezer for up to two months.
TO REHEAT: Heat the leftovers gently in a skillet or pan on the stovetop over medium heat until hot.

Air Fryer Bacon Wrapped Shrimp

Servings: 4
Cooking Time: 10 Minutes

Ingredients:
- 24 shrimp
- 1 tbsp Old Bay seasoning
- 8 pieces bacon thinkly sliced, cut into thrids.

Directions:
1. Peel the shrimp and set them aside in a single layer onto a baking sheet.
2. Sprinkle a small amount of Old Bay Seasoning over the peeled shrimp.
3. Cut the bacon pieces into thirds. Carefully wrap the bacon around the shrimp, taking care to tuck the bacon under the bottom of the shrimp.
4. Prepare the basket of the air fryer with olive oil or with a nonstick cooking spray.
5. Add the bacon wrapped shrimp to the basket of the air fryer. Take care to keep the bacon edge tucked under the shrimp.
6. Cook on 390 degrees for 9-10 minutes, or until fully cooked.
7. Carefully remove the shrimp from the air fryer and serve immediately.

Notes
Bacon wrapped shrimp are delicious all by themselves, but they are also delicious when served with Remoulade sauce, sweet chili sauce, bbq sauce, dijon mustard, or teriyaki sauce.

Air-fryer Fish Tacos

Servings: 4

Ingredients:
- 2 cups shredded green cabbage
- ¼ cup coarsely chopped fresh cilantro
- 1 scallion, thinly sliced
- 5 tablespoons lime juice (from 2 limes), divided
- 1 tablespoon avocado oil
- 1 large avocado
- 2 tablespoons sour cream
- 1 small clove garlic, grated
- ¼ teaspoon salt
- 1 large egg white
- ⅓ cup dry whole-wheat breadcrumbs
- 1 tablespoon chili powder
- 1 pound skinless mahi-mahi fillets, cut into 2- to 3-inch strips
- Avocado oil cooking spray
- 8 (6 inch) corn tortillas, warmed
- 1 medium tomato, chopped

Directions:
1. Toss cabbage, cilantro, scallion, 2 tablespoons lime juice and avocado oil together in a medium bowl; set aside.
2. Cut avocado in half lengthwise; using a spoon, scoop the pulp into the bowl of a mini food processor. Add sour cream, garlic, salt and the remaining 3 tablespoons lime juice; process until smooth, about 30 seconds. (Alternatively, mash with a fork to reach desired consistency.) Set aside.

3. Preheat air fryer to 400°F. Place egg white in a shallow dish; whisk until frothy. Combine breadcrumbs and chili powder in a separate shallow dish. Pat fish dry with a paper towel. Coat the fish with egg white, letting excess drip off; dredge in the breadcrumb mixture, pressing to adhere.
4. Working in batches if needed, arrange the fish in an even layer in the fryer basket; coat the fish well with cooking spray. Cook until crispy and golden on one side, about 3 minutes. Flip the fish; coat with cooking spray and cook until it's crispy and flakes easily, about 3 minutes. Flake the fish into bite-size pieces. Top each tortilla evenly with fish, avocado crema (about 1 tablespoon each), cabbage slaw (about 1/4 cup each) and tomato. Serve with lime wedges, if desired.

Air Fryer Tilapia

Servings: 3-4
Cooking Time: 10 Minutes

Ingredients:
- 4 tilapia fillets
- 2 tablespoons olive oil
- 1/2 teaspoon paprika
- 1/2 teaspoon garlic powder
- 1/2 teaspoon onion powder
- 1/2 teaspoon salt
- 1/2 teaspoon black pepper
- FOR SERVING (OPTIONAL)
- Lemon wedges

Directions:
1. Preheat your air fryer to 400 degrees.
2. Place the tilapia fillets on a large plate and drizzle with olive oil.
3. In a small bowl, mix the paprika, garlic powder, onion powder, salt, and pepper.
4. Sprinkle seasoning evenly over the fillets then place in a single layer in the air fryer.
5. Cook tilapia for 10 minutes, flipping the fillets halfway through cooking.
6. Remove the tilapia from the air fryer, serve with lemon wedges (if desired), and enjoy!

Notes
HOW TO REHEAT TILAPIA IN THE AIR FRYER:
Preheat your air fryer to 400 degrees.
Place leftover tilapia in the air fryer and cook for about 4 minutes, until heated through.
Remove them from the air fryer and enjoy!
HOW TO COOK FROZEN TILAPIA IN THE AIR FRYER:
Preheat your air fryer to 400 degrees.
Spray basket with cooking oil, place the frozen tilapia in the air fryer, and cook for about 13 minutes, until heated through, then enjoy!

Air Fryer Fish Tacos

Servings: 3
Cooking Time: 6 Minutes

Ingredients:
- 1 teaspoon garlic powder
- 1 teaspoon chili powder
- 1 teaspoon cumin
- 1/2 teaspoon kosher salt
- 1 cup Panko breadcrumbs
- 1 large egg
- 1 pound fresh cod filets cut in strips or pieces
- 8 small flour or corn tortillas
- Spicy Cream Sauce
- 1/2 cup mayonnaise
- 1/4 cup sriracha sauce
- 1 teaspoon fresh lime juice
- Optional Toppings
- 1 cup purple cabbage shredded
- 1 medium avocado sliced
- 1 cup cotija cheese crumbled
- 1 bunch cilantro garnish

Directions:
1. To prepare the air fryer basket, lightly spray with nonstick cooking spray, then set aside.

2. In a shallow medium bowl, add the garlic powder, chili powder, cumin, salt, and panko breadcrumbs. Stir together until well combined
3. In another shallow bowl, whisk egg. Dip each filet in the whisked egg, and then into the panko breadcrumb mixture. Be sure to coat both sides well.
4. Place filets in a single layer in the prepared air fryer basket and air fry at 350 degrees F for 6-7 minutes until golden brown.

Notes
Top Tips

I use thinner fish for this recipe. Add a few extra minutes to cooking time if using thicker fish filets.

To confirm doneness, use a fork to flake tilapia fish fillet to see if it easily flakes. To confirm proper temperature, use a meat thermometer to confirm doneness. It should be 130-135 degrees F.

I use fresh tilapia fillets for this simple recipe, but you can use frozen fish fillets as well. Add an additional 2-3 minutes to cooking process.

Air Fryer Shrimp Fajitas

Servings: 4
Cooking Time: 8 Minutes

Ingredients:
- 1 lb shrimp fresh shrimp, peeled, tails off, deveined
- 1 medium red bell pepper
- 1 medium orange bell pepper
- 1 medium green bell pepper
- 1 medium yellow onion medium
- 2 tbsp fajita seasoning mix
- Toppings:
- 1 small avocado sliced
- 1 teaspoon cilantro fresh, chopped

Directions:
1. Cut the onion and bell peppers into strips and place them in a medium bowl.
2. Rinse the shrimp under water in a colander and then place on a paper towel to pat dry. Add to the bowl with the shrimp.
3. Add the fajita seasoning to the shrimp and bell peppers and toss to coat them evenly.
4. Add the shrimp, peppers, and onion to the basket of the air fryer.
5. Air fry the shrimp and vegetables at 400 degrees Fahrenheit for 8 minutes, tossing the mixture halfway through the cooking process.
6. Carefully remove from the air fryer and serve on a flour tortilla and top with your favorite toppings.

Notes
This easy air fryer shrimp recipe can be served any way that you want. You can add the ingredients to a large bowl and top it with sour cream, cayenne pepper, and more. It's simple to turn this dish into air fryer shrimp fajita bowls.

You can also get flour tortillas or corn tortillas and fill them fully! Perfect for busy weeknights.

The best way to serve this recipe is to let everyone add their own toppings and enjoy.

Air Fryer Fried Shrimp

Servings: 4

Ingredients:
- Deselect All
- Fried Shrimp:
- 1 pound large shrimp (16/20 count), peeled and deveined, tails on
- Kosher salt and freshly ground black pepper
- 1/2 cup all-purpose flour
- 2 large eggs
- 1 cup panko breadcrumbs
- Nonstick cooking spray, for the shrimp
- Spicy Remoulade Sauce:
- 1/2 cup mayonnaise
- 2 tablespoons chopped pickled jalapenos
- 2 tablespoons whole grain mustard
- 1 tablespoon ketchup
- 1 tablespoon hot sauce
- 1 scallion, thinly sliced

Directions:

1. For the fried shrimp: Pat the shrimp dry between a couple paper towels, then season with a pinch of salt and a few grinds of pepper.
2. Whisk the flour with 3/4 teaspoon salt and few grinds of pepper in a shallow bowl or baking dish. Whisk the eggs with a pinch of salt in another shallow bowl. Add the panko to a third shallow bowl. Dip a shrimp in the seasoned flour, shaking off any excess, then dip in the beaten eggs. Dredge in the panko, turning until evenly coated. Transfer to a large plate or a rimmed baking sheet and repeat with the remaining shrimp.
3. Preheat a 5 quart air fryer to 385 degrees F. Working in batches, place some of the shrimp in a single layer in the fryer basket, then spray lightly with cooking spray. Cook, flipping halfway through, until the shrimp are golden brown and cooked through, about 10 minutes.
4. For the spicy remoulade sauce: Meanwhile, stir together the mayonnaise, pickled jalapenos, mustard, ketchup, hot sauce and scallion in a small bowl until smooth. Serve with the fried shrimp for dipping.
5. Cook's Note
6. You may need to fry the shrimp in 2 to 3 batches, depending on the size of your air-fryer basket.

Air Fryer Mahi Mahi

Servings: 3-4
Cooking Time: 12 Minutes

Ingredients:
- 1 to 1 1/2 pounds mahi mahi fillets
- 2 tablespoons olive oil
- 2 cups panko breadcrumbs
- 1 teaspoon paprika
- 1/2 teaspoon garlic powder
- 1/2 teaspoon onion powder
- 1/2 teaspoon salt
- 1/2 teaspoon pepper
- OPTIONAL
- Lemon wedges, for serving

Directions:
1. Preheat your air fryer to 400 degrees.
2. Place the mahi mahi fillets on a large plate and drizzle or baste with olive oil.
3. In a shallow dish, mix the panko breadcrumbs, paprika, garlic powder, onion powder, salt, and pepper.
4. Dip each mahi mahi fillet into the panko mixture then place in a single layer in the air fryer basket. Spritz with cooking oil.
5. Cook for 12 to 15 minutes, flipping the mahi mahi halfway through cooking.
6. Remove them from the air fryer, serve with lemon wedges, and enjoy!

Notes
HOW TO REHEAT MAHI MAHI IN THE AIR FRYER
Preheat your air fryer to 350 degrees.
Place the leftover mahi mahi in the air fryer and cook for about 3 to 4 minutes until heated thoroughly.
HOW TO COOK FROZEN MAHI MAHI IN THE AIR FRYER
Preheat your air fryer to 400 degrees.
Place the fillets in a single layer and cook for 13 to 14 minutes until heated thoroughly. Flip the mahi mahi halfway through cooking. If the fish is breaded, spritz with oil once at the beginning and once halfway through.

Air Fryer Breaded Shrimp

Servings: 4
Cooking Time: 8 Minutes

Ingredients:
- 1 pound large raw shrimp peeled and deveined (I use 31/40 size)
- 1 cup Italian Breadcrumbs
- ¼ cup grated Parmesan cheese
- 1/2 cup all purpose flour
- 1/3 cup water
- 1/2 tsp dried parsley flakes
- 1/2 tsp paprika
- ½ tsp salt

- ¼ tsp ground black pepper
- 1 large egg

Directions:

1. In a shallow bowl, add breadcrumbs, parmesan cheese, parsley flakes, paprika, salt and pepper. Stir with a fork to combine ingredients.
2. In another large bowl, add the flour, egg, and water. Stir together to make a liquid batter.
3. Toss shrimp with the flour and egg batter, until they are coated on both sides.
4. Dredge each piece of shrimp in the panko mixture, coating both sides.
5. Lightly spray the air fryer basket, and place each shrimp into the basket, without stacking or overlapping.
6. Lightly spritz the coated shrimp with olive oil and then place shrimp in the air fryer basket. Air Fry at 380 degrees F for 8-10 minutes, flipping shrimp halfway through air frying.

Notes

Variations

Use panko breadcrumbs - Instead of using regular bread crumbs, you can use Panko bread crumbs.

Change the seasoning - Use Old Bay seasoning, lemon pepper, red pepper flakes, Cajun seasoning, and any other flavors that you want to add to this shrimp recipe. The flavors take to the larger shrimp easily.

Make air fryer frozen shrimp - If you want to cook tender seafood, you can cook frozen shrimp in the air fryer as well. Just add them in a single layer in the basket of the air fryer.

Crisp-skinned Air Fryer Salmon With Salsa Verde

Servings: 4
Cooking Time: 25 Minutes

Ingredients:

- 4 x 185g salmon fillets, skin on
- 1 tablespoon extra virgin olive oil
- 2 teaspoon sea salt flakes
- 1 small shallot, chopped finely
- 1 clove garlic, crushed
- 2 teaspoon finely grated lemon rind
- 2 tablespoon lemon juice
- 2 tablespoon finely chopped dill
- ¼ cup chopped flat-leaf parsley
- 2 tablespoon chopped chives
- 1 tablespoon baby capers, chopped coarsely
- to serve: extra sea salt flakes

Directions:

1. Preheat a 7-litre air fryer to 200°C/400°F for 3 minutes.
2. Rub salmon with oil, then sprinkle with salt flakes.
3. Taking care, line the air fryer basket with a silicone mat, if available. Place salmon, skin-side up, in the basket; at 200°C/400°F, cook for 8 minutes until skin is crisp and salmon is cooked to your liking.
4. Meanwhile, to make salsa verde, combine remaining ingredients in a medium bowl; mix well. Season.
5. Serve salmon topped with salsa verde and sprinkled with extra salt flakes.

POULTRY RECIPES

Dry Rubbed Wings With A Gorgonzola Dipping Sauce

Ingredients:
- WINGS:
- 4 lbs chicken wings
- 2 Tbsp vegetable oil1/2 Tbsp ancho chile pepper
- 1/2 Tbsp onion powder
- 1/2 Tbsp kosher salt
- 3/4 Tbsp light brown sugar, packed
- 3/4 tsp chili powder
- 3/4 tsp cumin
- 3/4 tsp paprika
- 1/2 tsp cayenne pepper
- 1/2 tsp dried mustard powder
- 1/2 tsp garlic powder
- 1/4 tsp black pepper
- 1/4 tsp dried oregano
- 1/4 tsp dried ground thyme
- GORGONZOLA DIPPING SAUCE:
- 1/2 cup mayonnaise
- 3 Tbsp buttermilk
- 1/4 cup sour cream
- 3 oz crumbled Gorgonzola cheese
- 1 clove garlic paste
- 1/4 tsp black pepper
- 1/4 tsp kosher salt

Directions:
1. Preheat the air fryer to 380°F degrees.
2. Combine all dry rub ingredients in a small mixing bowl and set aside.
3. In a large mixing bowl, add the chicken wings and vegetable oil and toss.
4. Sprinkle in about half of the dry rub mixture and toss the chicken wings to coat evenly. Note: This dry rub mixture is enough for 4 lbs of chicken wings, but feel free to use all the dry rub or save the remaining for later.
5. Remove the air fryer basket and spray with canola oil spray if desired. Add the chicken wings to the basket.
6. Set the timer to 30 minutes and utilizing the ALARM feature, select the 15 minute option to remind you to flip the wings halfway through.
7. While the wings are cooking, make the gorgonzola dipping sauce. Add the mayonnaise, buttermilk, sour cream, gorgonzola cheese, garlic, pepper and salt. Mix and refrigerate until it's time to serve.
8. Once the wings are done, serve immediately with the dipping sauce and carrot and celery sticks. Enjoy!

Air Fryer Tandoori Turkey Breast

Servings: 4

Ingredients:
- 1 split skin-on, bone-in turkey breast (about 1 3/4 lb.)
- 1 1/2 tsp. kosher salt, divided
- 1 c. full-fat plain Greek yogurt
- 2 cloves garlic, minced
- 1 tbsp. sweet paprika
- 2 tsp. ground turmeric
- 2 tsp. minced fresh ginger (from a 1" piece)
- 1 tsp. ground cumin
- Olive oil cooking spray

Directions:
1. Pat turkey dry with paper towels; season all over with 1 teaspoon salt.
2. In a medium bowl, combine yogurt, garlic, paprika, turmeric, ginger, cumin, and remaining 1/2 teaspoon salt. Spread yogurt mixture all over turkey. Let stand at room temperature for 30 minutes.
3. Lightly coat an air-fryer basket with cooking spray. Place turkey in basket. Cook at 350°, flipping every 10 minutes, until turkey is golden brown and an instant-read thermometer inserted into thickest

part of breast registers 165°, 35 to 40 minutes. Let turkey rest about 10 minutes before slicing.

Air Fryer Whole Chicken

Servings: 6
Cooking Time: 44 Minutes

Ingredients:

- 3 lb whole chicken
- 2 tablespoons olive oil
- 1/2 teaspoon salt
- 1/2 teaspoon pepper
- 1 teaspoon smoked paprika
- 1 teaspoon Italian seasonings
- 1/4 teaspoon Rosemary
- 1/4 teaspoon mustard powder

Directions:

1. Preheat the air fryer to 180C/350F.
2. Pat dry the chicken, then drizzle the olive oil on all sides.
3. In a small bowl, combine all the spices. Rub the spices all over the chicken.
4. Place the chicken in the air fryer breast side down. Air fry for 25 minutes before flipping and cooking for a further 20 minutes. Once the chicken reaches an internal temperature of 165F, remove it from the air fryer.
5. Let the chicken rest for 5 minutes before carving.

Notes

TO STORE: Place leftover chicken in an airtight container and store it in the refrigerator for up to 5 days.
TO FREEZE: Once the chicken has cooled to room temperature, place in a ziplock bag and store it in the freezer for up to 3 months. You can also shred it before doing so.
TO REHEAT: Microwave portions of the chicken for 20-30 seconds or reheat in a preheated oven until warm.

Air-fryer Crispy Salt And Pepper Chicken Wings Recipe

Servings: 4
Cooking Time: 20 Minutes

Ingredients:

- 1kg-1.2kg pack Willow Farm chicken wings (about 16 wings)1kg-1.2kg pack Willow Farm Chicken wings (about 16 wings)
- 1 tsp sesame oil
- 1 tsp Shaoxing rice wine or Japanese mirin
- 30g plain flour
- ½ tsp white pepper
- ¼ tsp ground ginger
- sunflower oil spray
- 1 red chilli, thinly sliced
- 2-3 cloves of garlic, chopped
- 2 spring onions, thinly sliced
- For the dipping sauce
- 4 tbsp light mayo
- 100g natural yogurt
- 1 tbsp rice vinegar
- 1 tsp light soy sauce
- 1 tbsp caster sugar
- 2 tsp mild curry powder

Directions:

1. Preheat the air-fryer to 180°C.
2. In a large bowl, toss the chicken wings with the sesame oil and rice wine or mirin. Sprinkle over the flour, the white pepper, ground ginger, and some salt and black pepper, tossing until evenly coated.
3. Working in 2 batches, spray the basket of the air-fryer with a little oil and arrange half the chicken wings in a single layer with some space between them. Spray with oil and cook for 10 mins.
4. Tip into clean bowl and cook the next batch.
5. Put the sliced chilli, garlic and spring onion into the bowl with both batches of part-cooked chicken wings and shake to coat. Add everything from the bowl back into the air-fryer and cook for 10-15 mins, until dark golden brown and cooked through.

6. Meanwhile, stir together the ingredients for the dipping sauce, cover and chill for 10 mins before serving with the cooked chicken wings.

Air Fryer Chicken Katsu

Servings: 4
Cooking Time: 25 Minutes

Ingredients:
- 2 boneless skinless chicken breasts
- Kosher salt, to taste
- Black pepper, to taste
- 2 large eggs, beaten
- 1 tablespoon water
- 1 ½ cups Panko bread crumbs
- KATSU SAUCE
- 3 tablespoons ketchup
- 1 tablespoon Worcestershire sauce
- 1/2 tablespoon oyster sauce (or soy sauce), plus more to taste
- 2 teaspoons brown sugar
- SERVE WITH
- Steamed Rice
- Steamed Vegetables
- Katsu Sauce

Directions:
1. Dry the chicken breasts with paper towels, then use a sharp knife to cut them in half horizontally, creating four filets. If necessary, use a meat mallet to pound each portion to about ½-inch thickness. Season with salt and pepper, to taste.
2. Preheat the air fryer to 350 degrees F, spraying the inner basket with cooking spray.
3. In a wide, shallow bowl, whisk together the egg and water until well combined. To a second bowl, add the Panko bread crumbs.
4. Dredge the chicken in the egg, then press them into the bread crumbs, coating evenly. Repeat the process a second time with each piece, double coating them.
5. Place the chicken in an even layer in the air fryer basket, spraying the top with cooking spray.
6. Air fry for 16-18 minutes, carefully flipping the chicken halfway through and spraying with cooking spray before continuing to cook until golden brown and 165 degrees F internally. Repeat with the remaining pieces of chicken.
7. Transfer the katsu to a cutting board to rest for at least 5 minutes before slicing. Serve over rice, with vegetables and katsu sauce.

Air Fryer Whole Turkey With Gravy

Servings: 12
Cooking Time: 3 Hrs 15 Minutes

Ingredients:
- 14 lb. (6.35 kg) raw Whole Turkey
- 6 Tablespoons (90 g) butter , cut into slices
- 4 cloves garlic , sliced thin
- 1 Tablespoon (15 ml) kosher salt , or to taste
- black pepper , to taste
- Olive Oil (or oil of choice), to coat turkey
- 1 1/2 cups (360 ml) chicken broth
- 3/4 cup (95 g) all purpose flour (for the gravy)
- EQUIPMENT
- Halogen Air Fryer
- Instant Read Thermometer (optional)

Directions:
1. Thaw your turkey completely on the inside cavity. Remove and giblets and neck bones from the turkey cavity (many times the giblet pack will be tucked under the skin by the neck). Pat the turkey dry.
2. Tuck the butter slices and garlic in-between the skin and the turkey breasts. Rub olive oil over the turkey and season with salt and pepper.
3. Place the lower rack in the air fryer and spray with oil. Place the turkey breast side down in the air fryer. Pour in 1/2 cup of broth over the turkey. Place the extender ring and lid on the air fryer.
4. Air Fry the turkey at 350°F for about 2 1/2 to 3 hours.
5. Every 30 minutes, baste with chicken broth (the first 2 bastes will be with the remaining broth.

After that, baste from the broth & juices at the bottom of the air fryer).

6. After cooking for 2 hours, take off the air fryer lid and extender ring. Lift the turkey out, flip to breast side up, and then place back into the air fryer. Baste the turkey and then place the extender ring and lid back on
7. Continue to Air Fry at 350°F until the turkey reaches an internal temperature of 165°F at the thickest parts of the thigh, wings and breast, and the juices run clear when you cut between the leg and the thigh (about 30 minutes - 1 hour).
8. Let rest for about 15-20 minutes.
9. While the turkey rests, make the gravy. Remove the lower rack from the air fryer. Leaving the turkey juices and broth in the air fryer, skim the chunks from the drippings and broth.
10. Place flour in a medium bowl. Ladle in about 1 cup of the drippings and broth into the flour and whisk until smooth. Pour the flour mixture into the air fryer with the remaining drippings and broth. Whisk until smooth.
11. Place the air fryer lid back on and Air Fry at 400°F for 10 minutes or until thickened, whisking a couple times while cooking.

Air Fryer Doritos Crusted Chicken Strips

Servings: 6
Cooking Time: 25 Minutes

Ingredients:
- 9 oz. (255 g) Doritos or any flavor tortilla chips
- 1 large egg, beaten (or more if needed)
- 2 pounds (907 g) chicken, cut into thin strips
- 1 teaspoon (5 ml) garlic powder
- 1/2 teaspoon (2.5 ml) salt
- fresh black pepper, to taste
- For dipping: Ranch, sour cream, ketchup, bbq sauce or your favorite sauce
- EQUIPMENT
- Air Fryer

Directions:
1. Crush the Doritos or tortilla chips in a bag with a rolling pin. Crush them thoroughly. The smaller the pieces, the better they'll coat the chicken. Place the crushed chips in a bowl for dredging the chicken. Put the beaten egg in another bowl.
2. Season the chicken strips with garlic powder, salt and pepper.
3. Working with one or two chicken strips at a time, first coat the chicken strips with the egg, then coat with the crushed Doritos. Gently press the chicken into the crushed chips, then pour chip pieces over the chicken strips. Gently press chips into chicken. This help chips to stay dry. If they're wet, they stick less to the chicken.
4. Pre-heat your Air Fryer at 380°F (195°C) for 4 minutes. Spray the air fryer basket or racks with oil spray. Gently lay chicken pieces in the basket or on the racks in a single layer (cook in batches if needed). Spray oil spray on top of coated chicken.
5. Air Fry at 380°F (195°C) for 15 minutes. Gently turn the chicken pieces and spray the tops with oil spray (make sure to turn the chicken gently or else the chip pieces will fall off).
6. Air Fry for additional 3-5 minutes or until the crust is crispy golden brown and chicken is cooked through. Serve warm with your favorite dip.

Air Fryer Chicken Drumsticks

Servings: 5
Cooking Time: 25 Minutes

Ingredients:
- 5-6 chicken drumsticks
- 1/8 cup extra virgin olive oil
- 1/2 teaspoon garlic powder
- 1/4 teaspoon paprika
- 1/4 teaspoon onion powder
- 1/4 teaspoon salt
- 1/8 teaspoon pepper
- 1/2 cup BBQ sauce (I prefer Sweet Baby Ray's)
- OPTIONAL

- pinch of cayenne pepper to add spice

Directions:
1. Preheat your air fryer to 400 degrees.
2. Pat dry chicken drumsticks.
3. Mix together the olive oil, garlic powder, paprika, onion powder, salt and pepper, and cayenne pepper (if using).
4. Coat the chicken drumsticks with oil mixture and massage into the drumsticks for a few minutes to help keep the flavor in.
5. Add chicken drumsticks to the air fryer in one single layer and cook for 15 minutes.
6. Flip chicken and cook for another 5 minutes.
7. Baste chicken with BBQ sauce, flip, then baste other side of chicken with BBQ sauce.
8. Cook until chicken has an internal temperature of 165 degrees, about 3-5 more minutes.
9. Remove from the air fryer, baste additional BBQ sauce if desired and enjoy!

Cauliflower Rice Arancini

Servings: 2
Cooking Time: 25 Minutes

Ingredients:
- 1 Italian chicken sausage link (casing removed (2 3/4 oz))
- 2 1/4 cups riced cauliflower (frozen works great)
- 1/4 teaspoon kosher salt
- 2 tablespoons homemade marinara (plus optional more for serving)
- 1/2 cup part skim shredded mozzarella
- 1 large egg (beaten)
- 1/4 cup bread crumbs* (or gluten-free crumbs)
- 1 tablespoon grated Pecorino Romano or parmesan*
- cooking spray

Directions:
1. Heat a medium skillet over medium-high heat. Add the sausage and cook, breaking the meat up with spoon as it cooks as small as you can, about 4 to 5 minutes.
2. Add the cauliflower, salt and marinara and cook 6 minutes on medium heat, stirring until the cauliflower is tender and heated through.
3. Remove from heat and add the mozzarella cheese to the skillet and stir well to mix. Let it cool 3 to 4 minutes, until it's easy to handle.
4. Spray a 1/4 cup measuring cup with cooking spray and fill with cauliflower mixture, leveling the top. Use a small spoon to scoop out into your palm and roll into a ball. Set aside on a dish.
5. Repeat with the remaining cauliflower, you should have 6 balls.
6. Place the egg in one bowl and the breadcrumbs in another.
7. Add the parmesan to the crumbs and mix.
8. Dip the ball in the egg, then in the crumbs and transfer to a baking sheet. Spray the top with cooking spray.
9. If baking in the oven, bake 425F 25 minutes, until golden. If making in the air fryer, bake 400F for 9 minutes turning halfway until golden.
10. Serve with marinara sauce, for dipping.

Notes
half of the crumbs get tossed, the n.i. and smart points accounts for that.

Air Fryer Chicken Parmesan Recipe

Servings: 4
Cooking Time: 12 Minutes

Ingredients:
- 1/4 cup all-purpose flour
- 1/2 teaspoon garlic powder
- 1/2 teaspoon onion powder
- 1/2 cup panko breadcrumbs
- 2 ounces Parmesan cheese, grated (1 cup loosely packed or 1/2 cup store-bought)
- 2 large eggs
- 2 boneless, skinless chicken breasts (about 1 1/2 pounds total)
- 3/4 teaspoon kosher salt
- 1/4 teaspoon freshly ground black pepper

- Cooking spray
- 4 slices part-skim, low-moisture mozzarella cheese (about 4 ounces total)
- 1 cup store-bought or homemade marinara sauce
- Fresh basil leaves, for serving (optional)

Directions:

1. Place 1/4 cup all-purpose flour, 1/2 teaspoon garlic powder, and 1/2 teaspoon onion powder in a shallow bowl or plate and whisk to combine. Place 1/2 cup panko breadcrumbs and 2 ounces Parmesan cheese to a second shallow bowl or plate and whisk to combine. Add 2 large eggs to a third shallow bowl or plate and whisk to combine.
2. Slice 2 boneless, skinless chicken breasts in half horizontally (also known as butterflying). Season all over with 3/4 teaspoon kosher salt and 1/4 teaspoon black pepper.
3. Working with one piece of chicken at a time, coat the chicken in the flour mixture, then dip in the egg, letting any excess drip off. Coat in the panko-Parmesan crumbs. Place on a baking sheet or plate in a single layer.
4. Heat an air fryer to 400°F. Place 2 breaded chicken pieces in a single layer in the air fryer basket, making sure they do not overlap. Coat with cooking spray. Air fry until golden and crisp, 5 to 6 minutes.
5. Top each piece of chicken with a slice of mozzarella cheese, and secure each piece of cheese with 2 toothpicks. Air fry until the chicken is golden brown, an instant-read thermometer inserted into the center registers at least 165°F, and the cheese melts, 1 to 2 minutes more.
6. Transfer to a plate and cover loosely with aluminum foil. Repeat air frying the remaining chicken and cheese. When the second batch is almost ready, warm 1 cup marinara sauce on the stovetop over medium heat or in the microwave until warm.
7. To serve, remove the toothpicks, divide the marinara sauce evenly among serving plates, and nestle each serving of chicken Parmesan on top. Garnish with fresh basil leaves, if desired.

Recipe Notes

Storage: Refrigerate leftovers in an airtight container for up to 3 days.

Air Fryer Chicken, Broccoli, And Onions

Servings: 4
Cooking Time: 20 Minutes

Ingredients:

- 1 pound (454 g) boneless skinless chicken breast or thighs , cut into 1-inch bites sized pieces
- 1/4-1/2 pound (113-227 g) broccoli , cut into florets (1-2 cups)
- 1/2 onion , sliced thick
- 3 Tablespoons (45 ml) vegetable oil or grape seed oil
- 1/2 teaspoon (2.5 ml) garlic powder
- 1 Tablespoon (15 ml) fresh minced ginger
- 1 Tablespoon (15 ml) soy sauce , or to taste (use Tamari for Gluten Free)
- 1 Tablespoon (15 ml) rice vinegar (use distilled white vinegar for Gluten Free)
- 1 teaspoon (5 ml) sesame oil
- 2 teaspoons (10 ml) hot sauce (optional)
- 1/2 teaspoon (2.5 ml) sea salt , or to taste
- black pepper , to taste
- serve with lemon wedges , optional

Directions:

1. AIR FRYING OPTION #1: REGULAR COOKED BROCCOLI
2. Make Marinade: In a bowl, combine oil, garlic powder, ginger, soy sauce, rice vinegar, sesame oil, optional hot sauce, salt, and pepper.
3. In bowl add chicken. In a second bowl add broccoli and onions. Divide the marinade between the two bowls, stirring to coat each completely.
4. Air Fry: Add just the chicken to the air fryer basket/tray. Air Fry at 380°F/195°C for 10 minutes. Stir in the broccoli and onions with the chicken (make sure to include all the marinade). Continue

to Air Fry at 380°F/195°C for 8-10 minutes, or until the chicken is cooked through. Make sure to stir halfway through cooking so broccoli gets cooked evenly.

5. Season with additional salt and pepper, to taste. Add fresh lemon juice on top (optional) and serve warm.
6. AIR FRYING OPTION #2: EXTRA CRISPY, CHARRED BROCCOLI
7. Combine chicken, broccoli and onion in bowl. Toss ingredients together.
8. Make Marinade: In a bowl, combine oil, garlic powder, ginger, soy sauce, rice vinegar, sesame oil, optional hot sauce, salt, and pepper. Add the chicken, broccoli and onions to the marinade. Stir thoroughly to combine the marinade with chicken, broccoli and onions.
9. Air Fry: Add ingredients to air fryer basket/tray. Air Fry 380°F/195°C for 16-20 minutes, shaking and gently tossing halfway through cooking. Make sure to toss so that everything cooks evenly. Check chicken to make sure it's cooked through. If not, cook for additional 3-5 minutes.
10. If needed, season with additional salt and pepper, to taste. Add fresh lemon juice on top (optional) and serve warm.

Notes

Air Frying Tips and Notes:Shake or turn as directed in the recipe. Don't overcrowd the air fryer basket.Recipes were tested in 3.4 to 6 qt air fryers. If using a larger air fryer, the recipe might cook quicker so adjust cooking time.Remember to set a timer to shake/flip/toss as directed in recipe.

Butter Chicken

Servings: 6
Cooking Time: 30 Minutes

Ingredients:

- 1 ½ pounds boneless, skinless chicken breast, cut into 1-inch pieces
- Kosher salt, as needed
- 3 tablespoons ghee
- ½ cup shallots, thinly sliced
- 1 can fire roasted crushed tomatoes (28 ounces)
- 1 ½ tablespoons fresh ginger, grated
- 6 garlic cloves, minced
- 1 tablespoons ground fenugreek
- 2 ½ teaspoons kosher salt, plus more as needed
- 2 teaspoon ground paprika
- 2 teaspoons turmeric
- 1 teaspoon ground cumin
- ½ teaspoon ground cardamom
- ¼ teaspoon ground cloves
- 1/3 cup cashew butter
- 1 cup chicken stock
- 1 can coconut milk (15 ounces)
- 2 tablespoons fresh cilantro, chopped, for serving
- Warm naan bread, for serving
- Items Needed:
- Blender

Directions:

1. Season the chicken generously with kosher salt.
2. Select the Sauté Function on the Pressure Cooker and press Temp Set, then customize the temperature to high and time to 12 minutes.
3. Add 2 tablespoons of ghee into the pressure cooker, then sear off the chicken in batches, removing the chicken to a plate as each piece is golden brown on all sides.
4. Add the remaining ghee and the shallots into the inner pot and cook, stirring occasionally, until the shallots are translucent, then stir in the garlic, ginger, and spices, followed by the cashew butter. Pour in the tomatoes and chicken stock stir to dissolve the cashew butter, then add the chicken pieces back into the pot.
5. Place the lid onto the pressure cooker.
6. Select the Pressure function, adjust pressure to high, and time to 15 minutes, then press Start.
7. Slowly release pressure by sliding the vent switch in between Seal and Vent. Slide the switch to Vent after 15 minutes.

8. Open the lid carefully.
9. Stir the coconut milk into the sauce, then adjust the seasoning to taste with kosher salt.
10. Serve the butter chicken on plates with naan, garnished with cilantro.

Air Fryer Nashville Hot Chicken Hack

Servings: 2
Cooking Time: 20 Minutes

Ingredients:
- FOR THE CHICKEN:
- About 2-4 frozen pre-cooked breaded chicken breasts
- FOR THE NASHVILLE HOT SAUCE:
- 1/4 cup (60 g) butter
- 1/4 cup (60 ml) oil
- 1 Tablespoon (15 ml) ground cayenne pepper, or 2 Tablespoons for extra hot
- 2 Tablespoons (30 ml) brown sugar
- 1 teaspoon (5 ml) garlic powder
- 1 teaspoon (5 ml) paprika
- 1 Tablespoon (15 ml) Worcestershire sauce or soy sauce
- 1/2 teaspoon (2.5 ml) salt, or to taste
- 1 teaspoon (5 ml) black pepper
- FOR SERVING
- 6-8 slices (6-8 slices) white bread
- Pickles, whatever you prefer - bread & butter, dill, or both
- EQUIPMENT
- Air Fryer

Directions:
1. Make the Sauce: Combine all the sauce ingredients in a bowl or saucepan (butter, oil, cayenne pepper, brown sugar, garlic powder, paprika, Worcestershire or soy sauce, salt and pepper). Microwave or heat until butter is just melted (the hotter it is, the harder it will be to emulsify the spices in the liquids). Whisk thoroughly until smooth.
2. When the sauce is cooler, it doesn't separate as easily so we like to brush sauce on the chicken when the sauce is slightly cooler or room temperature. If you want your sauce warmer, then keep stirring or whisking the sauce as you brush the chicken so that you have as little separation of sauce/oil as possible. The warmer the sauce is, the more the spices will want to separate from the liquids.
3. Place the frozen breaded chicken breasts in the air fryer basket in a single layer. Make sure they aren't overlapping. No oil spray is needed.
4. Air Fry at 380°F/193°C for 10 minutes. Flip the chicken over.
5. Continue to Air Fry at 380°F/193°C for another 2 minutes. Check the chicken breasts and if needed, add another 2-3 minutes or until heated through and crispy to your preference.
6. Place chicken on top of white bread. Brush both sides of chicken with the hot sauce. Top with pickles and serve warm. Enjoy!

Notes
Air Frying Tips and Notes:
No Oil Necessary. Cook Frozen - Do not thaw first.
Don't overcrowd the air fryer basket. Lay in a single layer.
Recipe timing is based on a non-preheated air fryer. If cooking in multiple batches of chicken back to back, the following batches may cook a little quicker.
Recipes were tested in 3.7 to 6 qt. air fryers. If using a larger air fryer, the chicken might cook quicker so adjust cooking time.
Remember to set a timer to flip/toss as directed in recipe.

General Tso's Air-fryer Chicken

Servings: 4

Ingredients:

- 1 large egg
- 1 pound boneless, skinless chicken thighs, patted dry and cut into 1 to 1 1/4-inch chunks
- ⅓ cup plus 2 tsp. cornstarch, divided
- ¼ teaspoon kosher salt
- ¼ teaspoon ground white pepper
- 7 tablespoon lower-sodium chicken broth
- 2 tablespoon lower-sodium soy sauce
- 2 tablespoon ketchup
- 2 teaspoon sugar
- 2 teaspoon unseasoned rice vinegar
- 1 ½ tablespoon canola oil
- 3 - 4 chiles de árbol, chopped and seeds discarded
- 1 tablespoon finely chopped fresh ginger
- 1 tablespoon finely chopped garlic
- 2 tablespoon thinly sliced green onion, divided
- 1 teaspoon toasted sesame oil
- ½ teaspoon toasted sesame seeds

Directions:

1. Beat egg in a large bowl, add chicken, and coat well. In another bowl, combine 1/3 cup cornstarch with salt and pepper. Transfer chicken with a fork to cornstarch mixture, and stir with a spatula to coat every piece.
2. Transfer chicken to air-fryer oven racks (or fryer basket, in batches), leaving a little space between pieces. Preheat air-fryer at 400°F for 3 minutes. Add the battered chicken; cook for 12 to 16 minutes, giving things a shake midway. Let dry 3 to 5 minutes. If chicken is still damp on one side, cook for 1 to 2 minutes more.
3. Whisk together remaining 2 teaspoons cornstarch with broth, soy sauce, ketchup, sugar, and rice vinegar. Heat canola oil and chiles in a large skillet over medium heat. When gently sizzling, add the ginger and garlic; cook until fragrant, about 30 seconds.
4. Re-whisk cornstarch mixture; stir into mixture in skillet. Increase heat to medium-high. When sauce begins to bubble, add chicken. Stir to coat; cook until sauce thickens and nicely clings to chicken, about 1 1/2 minutes. Turn off heat; stir in 1 tablespoon green onion and sesame oil. Transfer to a serving plate, and top with sesame seeds and remaining 1 tablespoon green onion.

Air Fryer Chili Crisp Crunch Chicken Wings

Servings: 4

Cooking Time: 30 Minutes

Ingredients:

- 2 pounds (907 g) chicken wings
- Kosher salt , or sea salt, to taste
- black pepper , to taste
- garlic powder , optional
- 1/4 cup chili crisp crunch , or to taste
- OPTIONAL - FOR EXTRA CRISPY CORN STARCH CRUST
- 1/4 cup (30 g) corn starch , or as needed
- oil spray , as needed
- EQUIPMENT
- Air Fryer
- Oil Sprayer optional

Directions:

1. If you have whole wings, separate them into the drum and flat. If needed, pat dry the chicken wings. Season with salt, pepper, and optional garlic powder.
2. For oil-free version, place in even layer in air fryer basket/tray. Follow air fry instructions below. For Extra Crispy Crust, follow optional steps for corn starch crust.
3. FOR EXTRA CRISPY CORN STARCH CRUST
4. Add seasoning to the wings then lay them in single layer on a plate or cutting board. Sprinkle cornstarch over the wings on both sides.
5. Liberally spray wings evenly with oil spray so that all the cornstarch is coated in oil. There should be

no dry white clumps of cornstarch or else they will cook hard and dry.
6. Place the coated wings in your air fryer basket or tray/rack.
7. AIR FRY
8. Air Fry wings at 400°F/205°C for 20 minutes minutes or until crispy-looking and nearly cooked through.
9. Flip the wings and Air Fry at 400°F/205°C for additional 5-10 minutes or until wings are fully cooked and crispy.
10. Toss with the chili crisp/crunch to taste. Spiciness will vary greatly on the brand of chili crisp/crunch, as well has how much you use on the wings. Adjust to your preference.

Notes

No Oil Necessary. The wings have enough fat in the skin to crisp up nicely on their own.

Shake several times for even cooking.

Don't overcrowd fryer basket.

If using a sauce, it is added in just at the end, otherwise it often burns before the chicken wings are cooked.

Recipes were cooked in 3-4 qt air fryers. If using a larger air fryer, the recipe might cook quicker so adjust cooking time.

If cooking in multiple batches, the first batch will take longer to cook if Air Fryer is not already pre-heated.

Remember to set a timer to shake/flip/toss the food as directed in recipe.

Air Fryer Lebanese Chicken

Servings: 4
Cooking Time: 35 Minutes

Ingredients:

- 1 whole chicken 2-3 lbs cut up into 8 pieces
- 1 tbsp olive oil
- 2 tsp salt
- 1 tsp pepper
- 1 tsp ground coriander
- 1 tsp onion powder
- 1/2 tsp cumin
- 1/4 tsp cinnamon
- 1/2 large yellow onion cut into ½" pieces
- 3 cloves garlic grated
- 1/2 lemon juiced
- fresh chopped parsley garnish

Directions:

1. In a small mixing bowl, combine all of the spices- salt, pepper, coriander, onion powder, cumin, and cinnamon.
2. Place the chicken on a large mixing bowl and toss with olive oil. Then add the spice mixture and toss again to coat the chicken.
3. Add the chicken, onions, garlic, and lemon juice into a large ziplock bag and marinate for at least 30 minutes, up to over night.
4. Once the chicken has finished marinating, remove from the ziplock bag and place in the air fryer basket.
5. Air fry for 35 to 40 minutes at 350 F or until the thickest part of the chicken has reached an internal temperature of 165 F.

Notes

If there is moisture on the chicken, pat them dry with a paper towel before adding the oil and seasoning. Patting dry the chicken helps the seasoning stick much better.

You can easily turn this Lebanese chicken into a wrap or salad. After you air fry the chicken, allow it to rest before shredding the chicken to stuff into a warm naan or pita bread or place it overtop of a salad.

The easiest way to make sure the chicken is ready is by using an instant-read thermometer. The chicken should have an internal temperature of 165F. Be careful not to hit the bone when inserting the thermometer, as it'll lead to an inaccurate read.

If you have time, marinating the chicken overnight makes the chicken even more flavorful.

When placing the Lebanese chicken into the air fryer, place them in a single layer. Avoid stacking them as the chicken will steam instead of crisp up. If your pieces of chicken are on the larger side, you can air fry them in two batches.

Air Fryer 'kfc' Fried Chicken

Ingredients:
- Chicken:
- 8 pieces of free-range chicken – thighs and drumsticks (bone and skin on)
- 250ml buttermilk
- 1 free-range egg
- 1 Tbsp hot sauce (I use Cholula chipotle hot sauce)
- Flour coating:
- 2 cups flour
- 2 tsp salt
- 6 tsp dried herbs (thyme, sage, parsley, oregano, basil)
- 1 Tbsp celery salt
- 1 Tbsp fine white pepper powder (or a mix. Of black and white)
- 2 tsp Hot English mustard powder
- 1 Tbsp paprika
- 1 Tbsp garlic powder
- 2 tsp ground ginger
- Sunflower or canola oil for brushing / dabbing on the chicken

Directions:
1. Make the day before. Mix the buttermilk, egg, and hot sauce in a bowl and then add it to a Ziploc bag with the chicken. Seal and lay this flat in a dish overnight in the fridge.
2. Take the chicken out of the fridge at least an hour before you want to cook it so that it comes up to room temperature. Mix all the ingredients for the flour coating in a bowl until well combined.
3. Get a tray set out and lined with baking/silicone paper.
4. Dredge the chicken in the following order: Take the chicken from the buttermilk into the flour mixture and toss to completely coat then set aside on the lined tray. You could dab/brush a little oil over the chicken at this stage and then proceed to the next step but first tossing it into the flour. Once all pieces are coated, quickly dip, and coat each piece 2 – 3 more times each. If some of the flour mixture clumps don't worry, try and press it onto the chicken.
5. Dab the top of each piece generously with olive oil. I used a silicone brush.
6. Preheat your Instant Vortex / Duo Crisp to 180C/350F. When it reaches temperature, spray the basket with non-stick cooking spray or olive oil / neutral oil spray. It's ok to use an aerosol spray if you have one. Or brush lightly with sunflower or canola oil.
7. Carefully place the chicken pieces in the basket and cook for 24 minutes. Turn them over halfway at 12 minutes. They should be golden brown and crunchy. Cook for a few extra minutes if you like them to be a darker colour. Serve with coleslaw or any other condiment of your choice.

Air Fryer Chicken Bites With Parmesan Cheese

Servings: 4
Cooking Time: 18 Minutes

Ingredients:
- 2 teaspoons olive oil
- 2 teaspoons Worcestershire sauce
- 1 teaspoon dried Italian seasoning
- ½ teaspoon garlic powder
- ¼ teaspoon salt
- ⅛ teaspoon freshly ground black pepper
- 1 pound skinless, boneless chicken breast, cut into 1-inch cubes
- 2 tablespoons all-purpose flour
- cooking spray
- ¼ cup shredded Parmesan cheese
- 2 tablespoons chopped fresh parsley

Directions:

1. Whisk olive oil, Worcestershire, Italian seasoning, garlic powder, salt, and pepper together in a bowl. Add chicken cubes and stir to coat.
2. Preheat an air fryer to 370 degrees F (185 degrees C) for 10 minutes.
3. Add flour to the chicken mixture and stir to coat until all liquid is absorbed.
4. Place chicken in the basket of the air fryer and cook for 8 minutes. Using tongs, flip the pieces over. Spray tops with non-stick cooking spray and cook 8 minutes more.
5. Sprinkle Parmesan cheese and parsley over the chicken. Cook until cheese has started to melt, about 2 minutes more. Serve immediately.

Air Fryer Chicken Thighs With Salsa Verde And Lemony Kale Salad

Servings: 4

Ingredients:
- Deselect All
- Lemony Kale Salad:
- 3 tablespoons lemon juice
- 2 teaspoons Dijon mustard
- 1 teaspoon finely grated zest
- Pinch crushed red pepper flakes
- Kosher salt and freshly ground black pepper
- 5 tablespoons olive oil
- 1 bunch curly kale (about 10 ounces), woody stems removed and leaves very thinly sliced
- 1/2 cup panko
- 1 tablespoon finely grated Pecorino Romano, plus more for serving
- Chicken Thighs:
- Four bone-in skin-on chicken thighs (about 2 pounds total)
- 2 teaspoons finely grated lemon zest
- Kosher salt and freshly ground black pepper
- 1 tablespoon olive oil
- Salsa Verde:
- 2 teaspoons capers
- 2 oil-packed anchovy filets (optional)
- 1 clove garlic
- Kosher salt
- 1/4 cup plus 2 tablespoons olive oil
- 1 teaspoon red wine vinegar
- 1 teaspoon finely grated lemon zest
- 1 cup fresh parsley leaves, finely chopped
- 1 cup fresh basil leaves, finely chopped
- 1/2 small bunch chives, finely chopped (about 1/4 cup chopped)

Directions:
1. Special equipment: a 3.5-quart air fryer and a 6- to 7-inch round baking dish
2. For the lemony kale salad: Whisk the lemon juice, Dijon, lemon zest, pepper flakes, 1 teaspoon salt and several grinds of pepper in a large bowl until combined. Slowly whisk in 3 tablespoons of the olive oil until smooth and emulsified. Add the kale and toss until well coated. Taste and adjust the seasoning with salt and pepper, if needed. Set aside at room temperature to marinate and soften, at least 15 minutes at and up to 8 hours in the refrigerator.
3. Meanwhile, preheat the air fryer to 350 degrees F. Toss together the panko, remaining 2 tablespoons olive oil, a pinch of salt and a few grinds of pepper in a 6- to 7-inch baking dish until evenly combined. Place the baking dish in the air fryer basket and air fry until the panko are golden brown, stirring halfway through, 4 to 6 minutes. Remove the dish from the air fryer, stir in the Pecorino and set aside.
4. For the chicken thighs: Preheat the air fryer to 400 degrees F. Pat the chicken dry between a few paper towels (this will help the skin get crispy). Rub the lemon zest onto the skinless side of each thigh and season with a good pinch of salt and several grinds of pepper. Flip the thighs over, rub the olive oil onto the skin and season each thigh with a good pinch of salt and several grinds of pepper. Place the thighs in the air fryer basket skin-side up, leaving a little space between each piece. Air fry until the

skin is crispy and the chicken is browned all over and cooked through, 22 to 25 minutes.

5. For the salsa verde: Meanwhile, finely chop the capers, anchovy filets (if using), garlic and a small pinch of salt with a sharp chef's knife, mashing and scraping the mixture until it becomes a paste. Transfer to a small bowl and stir in the olive oil, vinegar and lemon zest. Fold in the parsley, basil and chives until thoroughly combined. Taste and adjust the seasoning with salt and pepper, if needed.
6. To serve, give the kale salad a good toss, then top with the toasted panko and some more grated Pecorino. Transfer the chicken thighs to a dinner plate or serving platter and spoon the salsa verde over the top. Serve with the kale salad.
7. Cook's Note
8. You can make the salsa verde in a food processor by pulsing together all the ingredients until the herbs are finely chopped and the sauce is just combined. (There's no need to chop the herbs first.)

Crispy Sesame Chicken

Ingredients:
- 1kg chicken pieces of your choice
- (I used drumsticks and chicken fillet)
- Salt and Pepper for seasoning
- 3 tablespoons cornflour
- 3 eggs
- 3 cups flour
- 3 tablespoons barbecue spice
- 3 teaspoon paprika
- 3 tablespoons sesame seeds
- 1 tablespoon mixed herbs
- Olive oil spray

Directions:
1. Cut the chicken fillets into strips and make 2 slits across the top of the drumsticks. In a medium bowl whisk together the egg with a dash of milk.
2. In a separate large bowl add together the flour spices, herbs and sesame seeds. Mix until well combined. Line a tray with baking paper or cling wrap. Rinse the chicken and pat dry with roller towel, season with salt and pepper and dust with the cornflour. Dip the chicken in the beaten egg and then in the flour mixture and transfer to the lined tray. Once all the chicken is evenly coated, transfer to the tray. Pop the chicken in the freezer for 20 minutes and allow the coating to set. (If you resting chicken for longer than 20 minutes pop the chicken in the fridge and not freezer)
3. After 20 minutes spray both sides of the chicken with olive oil and air fry in the Vortex Air fryer on 200 degrees for 15-20 minutes, turning halfway.
4. NB: To maximize crispness, do not overcrowd the basket, rather fry in 2 batches but leave enough space in between the chicken to crisp to perfection.
5. Enjoy!

Air Fryer Chicken Nuggets

Servings: 4
Cooking Time: 10 Minutes

Ingredients:
- 1 lb boneless skinless chicken breast
- 1/2 tsp salt
- 1/4 tsp pepper
- 1/4 cup flour
- 1/2 cup melted butter or 1 large egg
- 1/2 cup breadcrumbs
- 1/2 cup parmesan grated
- 1 tsp dried parsley
- olive oil spray
- Garnish:
- ketchup, bbq sauce, ranch dressing, or your favorite dipping sauce.

Directions:
1. Trim any excess fat from the chicken breast and cut the chicken into nugget-sized pieces. Season with salt and pepper.
2. Set out 3 shallow bowls. In the first bowl put the flour, in the second bowl put the melted butter or beaten egg.

3. In the third bowl, mix together the breadcrumbs, dried parsley, and parmesan cheese.
4. One at a time dip each piece of chicken in the flour first, then the butter or egg, and finally the breadcrumb mixture.
5. Once all nuggets are ready to cook, give them a light spray with olive oil and place them on a single layer in the air fryer. Cook for 7 minutes at 400F and then flip the nuggets. Cook for another 1 to 3 minutes at 400F until they are golden.
6. Serve with your favorite dipping sauce.

Notes

Make sure not to overcrowd the air fryer basket. The hot air needs to reach all the sides of the nuggets, so they crisp up.

Press the breadcrumbs onto the nuggets to help them adhere well. Doing so helps give the chicken a more even coating.

The key to cooking chicken nuggets in the air fryer perfectly is to ensure all the chicken nuggets are as uniformly as possible. You want them all to cook for the same amount of time.

After dipping the chicken nuggets, shake off any excess egg so the nuggets don't taste eggy.

Broccoli And Cheese Stuffed Chicken

Servings: 4
Cooking Time: 25 Minutes

Ingredients:

- 2 cups finely chopped broccoli floret
- 8 thin chicken breast cutlets (about 3 to 4 ounces each)
- 1 large egg
- 2 teaspoons water
- 3/4 cup whole wheat or gluten-free seasoned breadcrumbs
- 4 slices cheddar cheese (cut in half 3 oz)
- 3/4 teaspoon kosher salt
- olive oil spray
- toothpicks

Directions:

1. OVEN Directions:
2. Preheat oven to 425F. Spray a sheet pan with oil.
3. Place broccoli in the microwave with 1 tablespoon water, cover and cook 1 minute until soft. Drain and season with 1/4 teaspoon salt.
4. In a small bowl, combine egg, water and a little salt and beat with a fork; set aside. Fill a second bowl with breadcrumbs.
5. If the chicken isn't 1/4-inch thin, pound it thin with wax paper and a mallet. Season both sides of the chicken with 1/2 teaspoon salt. Place a 1/2 slice cheese in the center of the chicken and top with 2 tablespoons broccoli.
6. Roll the chicken around to completely cover cheese, using toothpicks to secure the ends, if needed.
7. Dip chicken into egg wash, then breadcrumbs and transfer to a sheet pan. Spray both sides of the chicken with oil and bake about 25 minutes, until cooked. Remove toothpicks and eat.
8. AIR FRYER RECIPE:
9. Preheat air fryer to 400F. Spray a sheet pan with oil.
10. Place broccoli in the microwave with 1 tablespoon water, cover and cook 1 minute until soft. Drain and season with 1/4 teaspoon salt.
11. In a small bowl, combine egg, water and a little salt and beat with a fork; set aside. Fill a second bowl with breadcrumbs.
12. If the chicken isn't thin enough to easily roll, pound it thin with wax paper and a mallet. Season both sides of the chicken with 1/2 teaspoon salt. Place a 1/2 slice cheese in the center of the chicken and top with 2 tablespoons broccoli.
13. Roll the chicken around to completely cover cheese, using toothpicks to secure the ends, if needed.
14. Dip chicken into egg wash, then breadcrumbs and transfer to a work surface. Spray both sides of the chicken with oil and transfer to the air fryer basket, in batches. Cook about 14 to 16 minutes, turning halfway until the chicken is cooked through in the center. Remove toothpicks before eating.

Air Fryer Buffalo Chicken Livers With Blue Cheese Dipping Sauce

Servings: 4
Cooking Time: 8 Minutes

Ingredients:

- 1 cup (2 sticks) butter
- ½ cup Hot Sauce
- 1 cup all-purpose flour
- 1 teaspoon salt
- ½ teaspoon paprika
- ½ teaspoon garlic powder
- ½ teaspoon cayenne pepper
- ½ teaspoon black pepper
- 1 pound chicken livers, soaked in milk
- oil, for spraying
- 1 cup blue cheese dressing
- 4 ounces blue cheese crumbled

Directions:

1. To make buffalo sauce, in a small saucepan, heat butter and The Lady & Sons Signature Hot Sauce until butter is just melted; keep warm until ready to use.
2. In a ziplock or paper bag, combine flour, salt, paprika, garlic powder, cayenne pepper, and black pepper. Place chicken livers in bag and shake gently until coated.
3. Working in batches of 10, spray each chicken liver with oil and place in air fryer basket. Do not overcrowd. Set temperature to 400 degrees, and air fry for 4 minutes. Turn livers, spray with oil, and air fry for 4 minutes more, or until golden brown. Transfer buffalo sauce to a large mixing bowl; in batches, immediately toss fried chicken livers in warm buffalo sauce. Repeat with remaining chicken livers.
4. To make dipping sauce, in a small bowl, stir together blue cheese dressing and crumbled blue cheese.

DESSERTS RECIPES

Homemade Strawberry Twists

Ingredients:
- 5 oz date paste
- 1.2 oz freeze-dried strawberries
- 3 scoops collagen peptides (optional)

Directions:
1. Soak dates for at least 30 minutes, up to eight hours. Drain and use a blender or food processor to blend until smooth.
2. Combine date paste, strawberries, and collagen powder (if using) into the food processor or blender.
3. Process the ingredients together until you have a thick fruit paste.
4. Prep your Air Fryer Oven trays with aluminum foil. We recommend poking small holes on edges to ensure that air can circulate.
5. Once you have your batter made, you can pipe it out onto trays.
6. Dehydrate the twists at 125 degrees F for 18-24 hours.
7. Store in an airtight container. Enjoy!

Zucchini Chocolate Chip Cookies

Servings: 2
Cooking Time: 10 Minutes

Ingredients:
- 1 1/2 c. all-purpose flour
- 1/4 tsp. kosher salt
- 1/4 tsp. baking soda
- 1/4 tsp. ground cinnamon
- 5 tbsp. butter, softened
- 1/2 c. granulated sugar
- 1/2 c. packed brown sugar
- 1 large egg
- 1/4 c. plain Greek yogurt
- 1 tsp. vanilla extract
- 1 c. shredded zuccini
- 1 c. semi-sweet chocolate chips
- 1 c. old-fashioned oats

Directions:
1. FOR OVEN
2. Preheat oven to 350°. In a small bowl, whisk together flour, salt, baking soda and cinnamon.
3. In a large bowl, beat together sugars and butter until light and fluffy. Add egg, yogurt, and vanilla and mix until evenly combined. Mix in flour mixture until just combined. Fold in oats, chocolate chips, and zucchini. Drop by rounded teaspoon 2 inches apart on baking sheets.
4. Bake for 15 minutes. Let cool for 2 minutes on baking sheet and transfer to wire rack to cool completely. Note: Cookies will spread a bit, but not take on much color.
5. FOR AIR FRYER
6. In a small bowl, whisk together flour, salt, baking soda and cinnamon.
7. In a large bowl, beat together sugars and butter until light and fluffy. Add egg, yogurt, and vanilla and mix until evenly combined. Mix in flour mixture until just combined. Fold in oats, chocolate chips, and zucchini.
8. Line air fryer basket with parchment paper. Working in batches, use a small cookie scoop to scoop dough and place on parchment paper at least 1" apart.
9. Cook at 350° for 10 minutes?! Remove cookies and let cool on a wire rack, and repeat with remaining dough. Note: Cookies will not spread much, but will get golden brown.

Air Fried Marshmallow Peeps

Servings: 4

Cooking Time: 5 Minutes

Ingredients:
- 1 package Marshmallow Peeps
- 1 Can Crescent Rolls 8 crescent rolls

Directions:
1. To make these peeps, begin by unrolling and separating each crescent roll.
2. Place one peep at the end of the crescent toll and roll until it is completely wrapped. Be sure to pinch any exposed parts of the peep.
3. Spray basket with nonstick cooking spray, or line with air fryer parchment paper. Place wrapped peeps in the prepared basket, leaving a small space in between peeps.
4. Air fry peeps at 350 degrees for about 5 minutes, until crescent rolls are golden brown
5. Carefully remove them from the Air fryer. Sprinkle with powdered sugar, drizzle with chocolate syrup or frosting glaze.

Notes

I make these in my Cosori 5.8 air fryer. Depending on size and wattage of the air fryer, you may need to add 1-2 additional minutes to cook time.

Leave enough room in between wrapped peeps, allowing room for the roll puff as it cooks.

Do not stack or overlap peeps in the basket. The dough may not cook evenly.

You can make 4 or 8 fried peeps in a batch, depending on what will fit in your basket.

Diet Friendly Avocado Brownies

Ingredients:
- 2 ripe avocados
- 4 eggs
- 1/2 butter (substitute: 1/2 cup coconut oil)
- 2 tsp vanilla extract
- 2 tsp baking soda
- 6 tbsp peanut butter
- 2/3 cup sugar (substitute: 2/3 cup Stevia)
- 2/3 cup unsweetened cocoa powder

Directions:
1. Add avocados, eggs, coconut oil, vanilla extract, baking soda, peanut butter, Stevia, unsweetened cocoa powder, and mix together in a blender or food processor.
2. Scrape the batter into a pan and smooth the top.
3. Place the pan in your air fryer, bake at 350 degrees for 15 minutes.
4. Enjoy!

Shrunken Apple Punch

Ingredients:
- 6 medium apples
- 1 gallon apple cider
- 4 cinnamon sticks
- 2 lemons
- 2 cups spiced rum/cinnamon whiskey (optional)
- Whole cloves

Directions:
1. Peel the apples and cut in half lengthwise. Scoop out the seeds and core.
2. Carve faces into the rounded side of the apple. Spritz with lemon juice to keep fresh.
3. Place apples face side up in the prepared sheet pan. Press cloves into the eye socket.
4. Bake at 250 for an hour or until the faces start to brown and dehydrate.
5. In a pressure cooker (or on stove top) add apple cider and keep warm.
6. When ready to serve, add the shrunken skulls to the cider.
7. Serve warm with 1 shrunken head.

Roasted Pears & Shortbread

Servings: 6

Ingredients:
- For the shortbread
- 65g unsalted butter, room temperature
- 30g light brown soft or light muscovado sugar
- 75g plain flour
- 15g cornflour
- Pinch fine sea salt
- For the roasted pears
- 6 (approx. 150g each) conference pears
- 2 small lemons
- 1 small orange
- 80ml honey
- 15g unsalted butter
- 2 tbsp water
- To serve crème fraîche

Directions:
1. Cream the butter, sugar and salt together in a bowl for about one minute. Combine the plain flour and cornflour together well before adding to the creamed mixture and mixing to bring together. Chill
2. before using
3. Pat the mixture out onto a piece of baking parchment to a rectangle shape 16cm by 12cm. Place on a tray and chill for for 20-30 minutes, or until firm
4. Squeeze one of the lemons into a bowl and add enough cold water to eventually cover the pears. Peel the pears and place into the bowl as you go. With a peeler, peel 3-4 strips on both the remaining lemon and orange. Squeeze both and add the juice to a small saucepan along with the peel, honey, butter and 2 tablespoons of water. Heat to just dissolve the butter
5. When the shortbread dough is firm, prick all over with a fork and cut into 6 rough squares
6. Remove the crisper plates from both drawers. Arrange the pears lying down in the Zone 1 drawer. Pour all the juice and honey mixture over them then insert drawer in unit. Place the 6 shortbread biscuits in Zone 2 drawer, making sure to leave space around them then insert drawer in unit. There is no need to grease the drawer as the buttery biscuits won't stick!
7. Select Zone 1, turn the dial to select ROAST, set temperature to 190°C and set time to 40 minutes. Select Zone 2, turn the dial to select BAKE, set temperature to 150°C and set time to 35 minutes. Press the dial to begin cooking
8. Carefully give the pears a turn and baste 2 to 3 times whilst they are cooking. Check that they are tender with a knife or you can roast them for longer
9. Remove the shortbread from the drawer with help of a small plastic spatula and place them on a rack to cool. The cooking juices can be reduced in a saucepan to desired consistency if necessary. Serve the pears and shortbread with crème fraîche

Air Fryer Fried Peach Pie

Servings: 4

Cooking Time: 10 Minutes

Ingredients:
- flour, for dusting
- one (8-ounce) package refrigerated crescent dinner rolls
- 4 tablespoons peach pie filling
- oil, for spraying
- ¼ cup prepared vanilla frosting

Directions:
1. On a lightly floured flat work surface, lay out 4 crescent roll triangles. Place 1 tablespoon of the peach pie filling in center of each triangle and cover with remaining 4 crescent roll triangles. Crimp edges with a fork to seal.
2. Working in batches of 2, spray both sides or pies with oil and air fry for 5 minutes. Turn pies, spray with oil, and air fry for 5 minutes more. Remove pies to a serving platter. Repeat with remaining pies.

3. In a small microwave-safe bowl, microwave frosting for 25 seconds. Drizzle pies with warm frosting.

Notes

Mix things up by using any pie filling that your family loves. Otherwise, follow the exact same instructions!

Air Fryer Donuts

Servings: 12

Cooking Time: 4 Minutes

Ingredients:

- 1 cup milk lukewarm (about 100°F)°
- 2 1/2 tsp active dry yeast or instant yeast
- 1/4 cup granulated sugar plus 1 tsp
- 1/2 tsp salt
- 1 egg
- 1/4 cup unsalted butter melted
- 3 cups all-purpose flour
- Oil Spray Coconut oil works best
- For the Glaze
- 6 Tbsp unsalted butter
- 2 cups powdered sugar
- 2 tsp vanilla extract
- 4 Tbsp hot water or as needed

Directions:

1. In the bowl of a stand mixer fitted with the dough hook, gently stir together lukewarm milk, 1 tsp of sugar, and yeast. Let it sit for 10 minutes until foamy (If nothing happens your milk was too hot or the yeast is too old, so start over).
2. Add sugar, salt, egg, melted butter and 2 cups of flour to the milk mixture. Mix on low speed until combined, then with the mixer running add the remaining cup of flour slowly, until the dough no longer sticks to the bowl. Increase speed to medium-low and knead for 5 minutes, until the dough is elastic and smooth.
3. Place the dough into a greased bowl and cover it with plastic wrap. Let rise in a warm place until doubled. Dough is ready if you make a dent with your finger and the indention remains.
4. Turn the dough out onto a floured surface, punch it down and gently roll out to about 1/2 inch thickness. Cut out 10-12 donuts using a 3-inch round cutter and a 1-inch round cutter to remove center.
5. Transfer donuts and donut holes to lightly floured parchment paper and cover loosely with greased plastic wrap. Let donuts rise until doubled in volume, about 30 minutes. Preheat Air Fryer to 350F.
6. Spray Air Fryer basket with oil spray, carefully transfer donuts to Air Fryer basket in a single layer. Spray donuts with oil spray and cook at 350F until golden brown, about 4 minutes. Repeat with remaining donuts and holes.
7. While the donuts are in the Air Fryer, melt butter in a small saucepan over medium heat. Stir in powdered sugar and vanilla extract until smooth. Remove from heat and stir in hot water one tablespoon at a time until the icing is somewhat thin, but not watery. Set aside.
8. Dip hot donuts and donut holes in the glaze using to forks to submerge them. Place on a wire rack set over a rimmed baking sheet to allow excess glaze to drip off. Let sit until glaze hardens, about 10 minutes.

Notes

Make sure the milk is not hotter than 115 degrees F. Using hot liquid will kill the yeast.

If you don't have an instant read thermometer, drizzle a few drops of the warmed up milk onto the inside of your wrist. It should feel warm. If it feels hot the yeast will die off, if it feels cold it will remain dormant.

Air Fryer Apple Chips

Servings: 1
Cooking Time: 10 Minutes

Ingredients:
- 1 Gala Apple
- 1-1 ½ teaspoon of cinnamon

Directions:
1. Wash and dry your apple.
2. Using a mandolin or a sharp knife, cut your apple into ⅛ inch slices.
3. Lay your apple slices into your air fryer basket. Sprinkle with cinnamon.
4. Place your basket in the air fryer and set the temperature to 360 degrees. Air Fry for 8-12 minutes, flipping at the 5 minute mark. Your smaller slices may come out before the larger slices; you just need to keep an eye on them. Once they are done cooking, let them sit in the basket for 5 minutes (place any you may have taken out back in) this will help them crisp up more.

St Patrick's Day Air Fryer Oven Chocolate Guinness Cupcakes

Ingredients:
- 2 cups all-purpose flour
- 1 teaspoon baking soda
- 1 teaspoon baking powder
- ¾ teaspoon salt
- 1 cup butter
- 1 cup Guinness stout
- ¾ cup special cocoa powder
- 1 tablespoon instant coffee granules
- 1 ½ cups granulated sugar
- ½ cup packed brown sugar
- 2 teaspoons vanilla
- 3 eggs
- ¾ cup sour cream
- 1 ½ cups butter, softened
- 4 cups powdered sugar
- 6 tablespoons Irish cream liqueur or caramel-flavor coffee creamer
- ⅓ cup caramel sauce
- ½ cup assorted green and/or gold sprinkles

Directions:
1. Line twenty-four 2 1/2-inch muffin cups with cupcake liners. In a large bowl whisk together flour, baking soda, baking powder, and 3/4 teaspoon salt, set aside.
2. In separate bowl, add 1 cup of hot melted butter, add in the room temperature Guinness, cocoa powder, instant coffee, and granulated sugar. Continue stirring until smooth.
3. In the bowl of an electric mixer, or hand held mixer, combine brown sugar and 1 teaspoon of the vanilla. Add melted butter mixture and beat on medium-low until cooled. Add eggs one at a time, beating after each addition until eggs are incorporated.
4. With mixer on medium, combine flour and batter mixtures. Once combined, add the sour cream, beating until combined and scraping down the sides of the bowl as necessary. Divide batter evenly among muffin cups. (They will be nearly full.)
5. Bake at 300 F for about 18 to 25 minutes or until a toothpick inserted in the centers comes out clean. Let cool in pans 5 minutes; remove to wire rack. Let cool.
6. Frosting:
7. For frosting: In the bowl of an electric mixer beat the softened butter on medium-high until creamy. Reduce speed; add powdered sugar, liqueur, caramel sauce, and the remaining 1 teaspoon vanilla. Increase speed to medium-high; beat until frosting is smooth and fluffy.
8. Pipe or frost cupcakes and add sprinkles. Makes 24 cupcakes. Enjoy!

Apple Cider Snickerdoodles

Ingredients:
- 1/3 cup apple cider
- 2 cups flour
- 1 tsp cream of tartar
- ½ tsp baking soda
- ½ tsp cinnamon
- ¼ tsp cloves
- ¼ tsp salt
- ½ cup unsalted butter, softened
- ½ cup granulated sugar
- 1/3 cup brown sugar
- 1 egg
- ½ tsp vanilla
- For Rolling
- ¼ cup granulated sugar
- 1 tsp cinnamon

Directions:
1. In a large mixing bowl, whisk together flour, cream of tartar, baking soda, cinnamon, cloves, and salt. Set aside.
2. In another large bowl, using a hand mixer beat the butter until smooth. Add both sugars and continue to beat until smooth.
3. Scrape down sides of bowl, add the egg and beat until just combined. Add the apple cider and vanilla and continue beating.
4. Add half the flour mixture and beat on low until combined then add the other half.
5. Tightly wrap the dough in plastic wrap and refrigerate for 2 hours.
6. Roll dough into 1 inch round balls, then coat in cinnamon and sugar. Place on baking tray and bake at 350 F for 8 minutes.
7. Let cool on a cooling rack.

Strawberry Pretzel Pie

Servings: 8

Ingredients:
- Pie Crust
- 1 cup fine pretzel crumbs
- 6 tablespoons butter, melted
- 2 tablespoons brown sugar
- 2 tablespoons maple syrup
- Items Needed
- 8-inch springform pan
- Stand mixer fitted with the paddle attachment
- Filling
- 16 ounces cream cheese, softened to room temperature
- ⅔ cup powdered sugar
- 1½ teaspoon vanilla extract
- ¼ teaspoon rose water
- 1½ cups heavy whipping cream
- ½ cup strawberry preserves
- 2 cups fresh strawberries, sliced, for garnish
- Fresh mint, torn, for garnish

Directions:
1. Place the pretzel crumbs, butter, brown sugar, and maple syrup in a medium bowl and mix until combined and the texture is like that of wet sand.
2. Pack the mixture into the bottom of an 8-inch springform pan.
3. Place the crisper plate into the Smart Air Fryer basket, then place the springform pan onto the crisper plate.
4. Select the Bake function, adjust time to 8 minutes, then press Start/Pause.
5. Remove the pie crust when done and let cool completely.
6. Place the cream cheese, powdered sugar, vanilla extract, and rose water into the bowl of a stand mixer fitted with the paddle attachment and mix on high until combined, then add the heavy whipping cream and continue beating until light and fluffy.

7. Remove the bowl from the mixer and stir in the strawberry preserves with a spatula to create a swirl throughout the batter.
8. Pour the filling into the cooled pie crust, then chill in the refrigerator for up to 2 days or until set.
9. Top the pie with fresh strawberries and mint before serving, then carefully remove from the springform pan, slice, and serve.

Easy Air Fryer Donuts

Servings: 10
Cooking Time: 10 Minutes

Ingredients:
- 1 can biscuits
- ¼ cup butter melted
- ½ cup sugar
- 1 tablespoon cinnamon

Directions:
1. Preheat air fryer to 350°F.
2. Cut a circle out of the center of each biscuit using a small 1" cutter.
3. Place 4-5 pieces of the dough in the air fryer.
4. Cook 3 minutes. Flip and cook an additional 2-3 minutes or until browned.
5. Remove from the air fryer and while warm, brush with butter. Combine sugar & cinnamon, toss donuts in sugar mixture.
6. Repeat with remaining donuts. Once the donuts are cooked, add the donut holes to the air fryer and cook for 3 minutes. Toss with additional butter and sugar if desired.

Notes
If you don't have a 1" cutter, the center can be cut using a large pastry tip.
Donuts can be cooled and glazed or dipped in glaze if preferred.

Red Velvet Cake Parfaits

Ingredients:
- 1 Red Velvet Cake Mix
- 1 cup water
- 1/3 cup vegetable oil
- 3 eggs
- For the custard filling:
- 8oz cream cheese, softened
- 1/2 stick butter
- 3/4 cup half and half
- 1 cup powdered sugar
- 1/2 cup sour cream
- 1/4 cup milk
- 1/2 tsp vanilla

Directions:
1. In a mixing bowl, combine cake mix with the water, oil and eggs. Whisk until smooth.
2. Grease an air fryer baking pan and pour the red velvet mix in.
3. Place the baking pan inside the basket of the Steam Air Fryer. Fill the Water Tank with water.
4. Set your Air Fry cook at 350° F for 15 minutes, then press the Mode Button once to set
5. your Steam cook at 212° F for 10 minutes. Press the Mode Button again to select the Combo cooking mode and begin the cooking cycle.
6. Once the cake is finished, set aside to cool.
7. In a mixing bowl, beat together cream cheese, butter, and half and half. Beat until smooth. While continuing to beat, gradually add the powdered sugar. Beat in the sour cream, milk and vanilla. Will resemble a custard consistency.
8. Using a fork, crumble the cake.
9. In the glasses of your choosing, assemble the parfaits by adding the crumbled cake in a 1 inch layer and the custard filling. Repeat the layering process until the glasses are filled.
10. Top with whipped topping, sprinkles or chocolates. Enjoy!

Air-fryer Hot-cross-bun Ice-cream Balls

Servings: 4
Cooking Time: 10 Minutes

Ingredients:
- 500g vanilla ice-cream
- 1 pkt traditional hot cross buns
- 3 free range eggs
- 2 cups milk
- 5ml extra virgin olive oil cooking spray
- 1 cup caramel fudge topping
- 125g raspberries
- 2 bananas, sliced

Directions:
1. Line a baking tray with baking paper. Scoop ice-cream into 4 large walnut-sized balls. Place on tray and freeze for 2 hours or until very firm.
2. Roughly tear hot cross buns into pieces and then process until fine crumbs form.
3. Place on a large flat plate. Whisk eggs and milk in a large bowl.
4. Working quickly with one ball at a time, using 2 forks to hold ice-cream, dip in egg mixture then roll in hot-cross-bun crumbs to thickly coat, making sure ice-cream is completely covered in a thick layer of crumb. Then repeat to double crumb.
5. Place on tray and freeze for 4 hours or overnight until very firm.
6. Line basket of a 4L air fryer with baking paper. Spray ice-cream balls with cooking oil, then place in the air-fryer basket. Cook for 2-3 minutes on 200°C, or until golden brown and crisp. Carefully transfer balls to serving bowls. Drizzle with topping and serve with raspberries and banana.

Air Fryer Blueberry Scones

Servings: 16
Cooking Time: 6 Minutes

Ingredients:
- 1/3 cup butter slightly softened
- 1 3/4 cups all purpose flour
- 1/4 cup sugar
- 2 teaspoon baking powder
- 1 large egg
- 3/4 cup fresh or frozen blueberries
- 4 tablespoon milk

Directions:
1. In a medium bowl, combine the butter, flour, sugar, and baking powder. Stir until it become crumbly.
2. Add in the egg, and the milk, one tablespoon at a time, until the dough forms.
3. Stir in the blueberries.
4. Roll the dough, until it is about ½ inch thick. Cut with 2 inch cutter.
5. Place in air fryer basket on parchment paper, or lightly brushed with olive oil.
6. Cook at 380 degrees Fahrenheit for 5-6 minutes, until they are golden.

Notes

Do not use air fryer with just parchment paper by itself. It must be weighted down by the, or it can be a fire hazard!

Caramelized Banana Pudding Cups

Servings: 4
Cooking Time: 6 Minutes

Ingredients:
- 1 tablespoon brown sugar
- 2 bananas, peels on, halved lengthwise
- 2 cups frozen whipped topping or dairy free frozen whipped topping
- 12 vanilla wafer cookies, broken
- Items Needed:
- 4 serving glasses

Directions:

1. Sprinkle the brown sugar onto the cut side of the banana halves.
2. Select the Preheat function on the Air Fryer, adjust the temperature to 400°F, then press Start/Pause.
3. Place the banana halves cut side up into the preheated air fryer basket.
4. Set temperature to 400°F and time to 6 minutes, then press Start/Pause.
5. Remove the bananas halves when done and scoop the fruit into a bowl, discarding the peels.
6. Add half of the whipped topping to the bananas and mash together.
7. Place a layer of broken cookies at the bottom of each serving glass topped with a layer of the banana mixture, followed by the whipped topping. Repeat.
8. Serve immediately or chill for up to 24 hours.

Air Fryer Mint Aero Danish

Servings: 4
Cooking Time: 10 Minutes

Ingredients:

- 2 sheets frozen puff pastry, thawed
- 118g block Aero mint chocolate
- Thickened cream, to serve (optional)
- Select all Ingredients:

Directions:

1. Place 1 sheet of puff pastry on a flat working surface. Using an assortment of different-sized round cookie cutters, cut rounds from pastry, discarding trimmings.
2. Cut the remaining pastry sheet in half. Place the chocolate in the centre of 1 half of the pastry sheet. Brush the edges with a little cream and place the second half of the pastry sheet on top. Press the edges to seal. Brush with a little cream. Working with 1 pastry round at a time, place it over the top, pressing gently to secure to pastry. Repeat with remaining pastry rounds to form a decorative pattern. Trim pastry, leaving a 1cm border around chocolate.
3. Place in an air fryer and cook at 200C for 10 minutes or until crisp and golden. Turn air fryer off and let pastry sit for a further 5 minutes (this helps make the chocolate soft and gooey).
4. Cut into slices and serve with cream, if using.

Frozen Grands Biscuits In Air Fryer

Servings: 6
Cooking Time: 22 Minutes

Ingredients:

- 6 Frozen Grands Biscuits
- oil spray
- butter and/or jam , optional

Directions:

1. Spray the air fryer basket or racks with oil to keep the biscuits from sticking. We don't suggest using parchment paper underneath because you want maximum air flow under the biscuits to help them cook all the way though. The parchment paper prevents maximum air flow under the biscuits.
2. Lay biscuits in single layer of air fryer basket or racks. Make sure to space them out so they aren't touching & have room to rise & expand. Cook in batches if needed.
3. Spray the tops of the biscuits to give them a more golden top when they air fry.
4. Air Fry at 330°F/165°C for 10 minutes. Gently wiggle the biscuits to loosen from the baskets. Flip the biscuits over.
5. Continue to Air Fry at 330°F/165°C for another 8-12 minutes, or until golden and cooked through. If they're still slightly doughy in the middle, leave them in the turned-off air fryer for about 2-3 minutes to continue cooking in the residual heat. Serve with butter or jam if desired.

Air-fryer Apple Fritters

Servings: 15
Cooking Time: 10 Minutes

Ingredients:
- 1-1/2 cups all-purpose flour
- 1/4 cup sugar
- 2 teaspoons baking powder
- 1-1/2 teaspoons ground cinnamon
- 1/2 teaspoon salt
- 2/3 cup 2% milk
- 2 large eggs, room temperature
- 1 tablespoon lemon juice
- 1-1/2 teaspoons vanilla extract, divided
- 2 medium Honeycrisp apples, peeled and chopped
- Cooking spray
- BROWNED BUTTER GLAZE:
- 1/4 cup butter
- 1 cup confectioners' sugar
- 1 tablespoon 2% milk

Directions:
1. Preheat air fryer to 410°. In a large bowl, combine flour, sugar, baking powder, cinnamon and salt. Add milk, eggs, lemon juice and 1 teaspoon vanilla extract; stir just until moistened. Fold in apples.
2. Line air-fryer basket with parchment (cut to fit); spritz with cooking spray. In batches, drop dough by 1/4 cupfuls 2 in. apart onto parchment. Spritz with cooking spray. Cook until golden brown, 5-6 minutes. Turn fritters; continue to air-fry until golden brown, 1-2 minutes.
3. Melt butter in small saucepan over medium-high heat. Carefully cook until butter starts to brown and foam, about 5 minutes. Remove from heat; cool slightly. Add confectioners' sugar, 1 tablespoon milk and remaining 1/2 teaspoon vanilla extract to browned butter; whisk until smooth. Drizzle over fritters before serving.

Air Fryer Oatmeal Cookies

Servings: 24
Cooking Time: 9 Minutes

Ingredients:
- ½ cup butter softened
- ¼ cup sugar
- ½ cup packed brown sugar
- 1 egg large, room temperature
- ½ teaspoon vanilla
- 1 ½ cups quick-cooking oats
- ¾ cup all-purpose flour + 2 tablespoons
- ½ teaspoon baking soda
- 1 teaspoon salt
- ½ teaspoon cinnamon
- ½ cup chocolate chips
- ½ cup raisins

Directions:
1. Preheat air fryer to 325°F without parchment paper.
2. Cream butter and sugar in a bowl with a hand mixer. Beat in egg and vanilla.
3. Combine oats, flour, baking soda, cinnamon, and salt in a bowl. Add a bit at a time to the egg mixture.
4. Fold in chocolate chips and raisins.
5. Place tablespoons of cookie dough on a small piece of parchment paper in the air fryer basket about 1" apart.
6. Air fry for 6-9 minutes or just until golden on the edges. Repeat with remaining dough, subsequent batches may take 1 minute less.

Notes
For high-rising cookies, avoid overmixing the dough. Chill the dough for 30 minutes before air frying so the cookies spread evenly.

Basque Burnt Cheesecake

Servings: 8-10
Cooking Time: 33 Minutes

Ingredients:
- 750g Full Fat Cream Cheese
- 200g Castor Sugar
- 4 eggs
- 1 egg yolk
- 1 ½ Cups Cream
- Generous ½ Tsp sea salt
- 1tsp Vanilla Extract
- 30g Cake Flour
- Zest of 1 Orange (optional)
- Butter for greasing the cake tin
- Baking paper for lining the cake tin

Directions:
1. Lightly butter the cake tin with a knob of butter. Cut two large squares of baking paper, big enough to hang over the sides of the tin. Line the tin with the 2 overlapping pieces of baking paper, making sure parchment comes at least 5cm above the top of the cake tin on all sides. Push the parchment into the corners of the tin. The pleats and creases of the baking paper will result in the edges of the cheesecake being a little pleated - but don't worry about this as this is a break the rules cheesecake.
2. Place the cream cheese and sugar into a bowl and beat until smooth, for 1-2 minutes on medium-high speed, scraping down the sides of the bowl as you go, until the sugar has dissolved. Turn the mixer to medium and add the eggs and egg yolk one at a time, beating well between each addition,. Scrape the sides of the bowl then give everything a further beat on medium.
3. Add the cream, salt, vanilla, and beat until combined.
4. Sift the flour over the cheesecake batter, and beat one final time until the flour is just incorporated into the batter (don't over beat). Pour the batter into the lined cake tin.
5. Set the Instant Vortex to 191C, for 33 minutes on the bake function. Once preheated, place the cheesecake into the basket, and cook until the top is a deep dark brown. At 28 minutes check the cheesecake, it should be jiggly in the center, as if undercooked. If the middle is still wobbly, the cake is ready, if not pop it back into the basket and check in another minute or two.
6. Once cooked, remove the cheesecake and allow it to cool to room temperature. The set of the cheesecake will be custardy, with a very loose center even once cool. The center should just hold a cut once cooled.
7. Serve the cheesecake at room temperature with a glass of sherry.
8. If making the cheesecake in advance, store it wrapped in the fridge, then remove it from the fridge 2 hours before serving, to achieve the ideal creamy texture at room temp.

Baked Apple Cider Donuts

Ingredients:
- 1 cup apple cider, reduced to ½ cup
- 1 ½ cups flour
- 1 ½ tsp baking powder
- 1 tsp cinnamon
- ¼ tsp ground nutmeg
- 1/8 tsp ground cloves
- ¼ tsp salt
- ¼ cup Greek yogurt
- ½ cup brown sugar
- 1 egg
- 1 tsp vanilla extract
- 3 Tbsp unsalted butter, melted and slightly cooled
- For the cinnamon sugar coating
- 4-6 Tbsp unsalted butter
- ¾ cup granulated sugar
- 2 tsp cinnamon

Directions:
1. For the Apple Cider Donuts

2. Spray the silicone mini muffin pan silicone with non-stick cooking spray.
3. Add the apple cider in a saucepan and bring to a boil for 7-10 minutes or until the cider has reduced to ½ cup. Remove from the heat and let cool.
4. In a large mixing bowl, whisk together the flour, baking powder, cinnamon, nutmeg, cloves, and salt. Set aside.
5. In a separate bowl, mix together the cooled reduced apple cider, Greek yogurt, brown sugar, egg, vanilla, and melted butter until fully combined. Add the dry ingredients and mix until well combined.
6. Fill each muffin cavity halfway.
7. Bake at 350 F for 8 minutes. Remove silicone mini muffin pan from the Air Fryer, flip each donut and place back in to cook for another 5 minutes.
8. For the cinnamon sugar coating
9. Add the melted butter to a small heatproof bowl and set aside. Start with 4 Tbsp and melt 1-2 more Tbsp of butter if needed.
10. In a separate bowl, mix the sugar and cinnamon until well combined. Take each donut and dunk it in the melted butter, or brush with silicone brush. Then roll in the cinnamon sugar mixture making sure to coat well. Repeat until all donuts are coated.

BREAKFAST & BRUNCH RECIPES

Air Fryer Cinnamon Roll Bites

Servings: 4
Cooking Time: 6 Minutes

Ingredients:
- 1 can cinnamon rolls I use Pillsbury

Directions:
1. Open the canned cinnamon rolls, remove the icing to a small bowl, and set it aside.
2. Use a knife to cut the cinnamon rolls into equal pieces. Take each piece of cinnamon roll and hand roll it until they are small round dough balls.
3. Place the cinnamon roll bites in a single layer into the prepared basket of the air fryer.
4. Air fry cinnamon rolls at 320 degrees Fahrenheit for 6 minutes or until golden brown, flipping the bites halfway through.
5. Carefully remove the cinnamon roll bites from the air fryer basket and serve with the icing as a dipping sauce.

Notes

I make this recipe in my Cosori 5.8 qt. air fryer or 6.8 quart air fryer. Depending on your air fryer, size and wattages, cooking time may need to be adjusted 1-2 minutes.

Store remaining bites in an airtight container in the refrigerator for up to 3 days. To reheat, add the cinnamon bites back to the air fryer and reheat at 320 degrees Fahrenheit for 1-2 minutes, or until they are heated through.

Air Fryer Lasagna Egg Rolls

Servings: 15
Cooking Time: 30 Minutes

Ingredients:
- 3 cups (710 ml) cooked lasagna, cooled
- 1 cup (112 g) shredded mozzarella cheese
- 15 (15) egg roll wrappers
- water, for sealing the wrappers
- oil spray, for coating the egg rolls
- 1/2-1 cup (120-240 ml) dipping sauce of choice, marinara, ranch, bbq sauce, etc.
- EQUIPMENT
- Air Fryer

Directions:
1. Cook the lasagna and then let cool to at least room temperature or use leftover lasagna. Cut into small slices about 2 Tablespoons in volume.
2. Using egg roll wrappers or spring roll wrappers, add the 2 Tablespoons piece of the lasagna filling to each wrapper. Add about 2 teaspoons of shredded cheese on top. Tuck and roll the wrapper around the filling (watch the video in the post above to see how to roll even and tight rolls). Brush the top corner of the wrapper with water to help seal the wrapper end, and then finish rolling the egg roll. Repeat for all the egg rolls.
3. Brush or spray rolls with oil to coat. Place egg rolls in a single layer in the air fryer basket (cook in batches).
4. Air Fry 380°F for 12-16 minutes, flipping halfway through. Cook until the wrapper is crispy and browned. If you use the larger wrapper or if your wrappers are thicker cook a little longer so that all the layers can cook through to avoid being tough and chewy.
5. Allow to cool a little (the filling will be super hot right after cooking), and then serve with your favorite dipping sauce.

Air Fryer "pretzel" Bites & Irish Pub Beer Cheese

Servings: 6

Ingredients:
- Pretzel Bites:
- 1 can prepared biscuits
- 8 cups water
- ⅓ cup baking soda
- ¼ cup butter, melted
- 2 tablespoons flaky salt or pretzel salt
- Items Needed:
- Slotted spoon
- Food processor fitted with blade attachment
- Small heatproof baking dish
- Beer Cheese:
- 6 ounces cream cheese
- 1 cup sharp cheddar cheese, freshly shredded
- 1 cup Irish cheddar cheese, freshly shredded
- 1 cup Fontina cheese, freshly shredded
- ⅔ cup stout beer
- 3 garlic cloves, minced
- 1 tablespoon spicy brown mustard
- 1½ teaspoons Worcestershire sauce
- 1 teaspoon paprika
- 1 teaspoon kosher salt
- 1 tablespoon fresh chives, chopped, for garnish

Directions:
1. Cut the individual biscuits into quarters and roll into balls. Set aside.
2. Bring the water to a boil in a large saucepan and add the baking soda. Boil the biscuit dough balls for 15 to 20 seconds at a time, then transfer to a tray using a slotted spoon.
3. Place the crisper plate into the Smart Air Fryer basket, then place the boiled dough balls onto the crisper plate in a single layer.
4. Brush the dough balls with melted butter and sprinkle with flaky salt or pretzel salt.
5. Select the Air Fry function, adjust time to 10 minutes, then press Start/Pause. Open the basket to brush the pretzel bites with butter every 3 to 4 minutes.
6. Remove the pretzel bites when done.
7. Place the cream cheese and all three shredded cheeses into the bowl of a food processor fitted with the blade attachment. Blend until fully combined.
8. Add the beer, garlic, mustard, Worcestershire sauce, paprika, and salt into the food processor and blend until smooth.
9. Transfer the cheese into a small heatproof baking dish.
10. Place the baking dish onto the crisper plate.
11. Select the Broil function, adjust time to 5 minutes, then press Start/Pause.
12. Remove the beer cheese when done, garnish with chives, and serve with the pretzel bites.

Air Fryer French Toast Sticks

Servings: 4

Cooking Time: 10 Minutes

Ingredients:
- 5 slices of bread
- 2 eggs
- 1/3 cup milk
- 3 tablespoons sugar
- 2 tablespoons flour
- 1 teaspoon ground cinnamon
- 1/2 teaspoon vanilla extract
- 1/8 teaspoon salt
- OPTIONAL
- Confectioners sugar for dusting
- Maple syrup for dipping

Directions:
1. Preheat your air fryer to 370 degrees.
2. Cut each piece of bread into 3 equal pieces and set aside.
3. Put the eggs, milk, flour, sugar, vanilla, ground cinnamon, and salt into a wide shallow dish. Whisk to combine.
4. Dip each piece of bread into the egg mixture, making sure to coat on all sides.

5. Place a piece of parchment round paper inside the air fryer and place each french toast stick in one single layer on top of the parchment round (needed to prevent sticking).
6. Cook for about 10 minutes, flipping halfway through.
7. Carefully remove the air fryer french toast sticks from the air fryer and enjoy immediately, store in the fridge for up to 3 days, or freeze up to 3 months.

Notes

HOW TO REHEAT FRENCH TOAST STICKS IN THE AIR FRYER:
Preheat your air fryer to 350 degrees.
Cook french toast sticks for 2-3 minutes until warmed and enjoy!
HOW TO COOK FROZEN FRENCH TOAST STICKS IN THE AIR FRYER:
Preheat your air fryer to 320 degrees.
Cook frozen french toast sticks in the air fryer for 2-3 minutes until warmed and enjoy!

Air Fryer French Onion Corn On The Cob

Servings: 4
Cooking Time: 25 Minutes

Ingredients:
- 4 corn on the cob
- mayonnaise, to taste
- French onion soup mix, to taste
- dry ranch dressing mix, to taste
- garlic powder, to taste
- black pepper , to taste
- paprika, to taste

Directions:
1. Mix all ingredients, except the corn, together in a bowl. Coat each cob with the mixture and individually
2. wrap each one in aluminum foil. Air fry it at 350°F for 20-25 minutes.
3. You can also bake it in the oven at 375°F for 25 minutes or grill it until the corn is tender.

Air Fryer Croutons

Servings: 6
Cooking Time: 10 Minutes

Ingredients:
- 7 slices bread
- 1 tablespoon olive oil
- ⅛ teaspoon salt
- ⅛ teaspoon pepper

Directions:
1. Preheat air fryer to 350°F.
2. Cut bread into medium sized cubes.
3. Toss with olive oil and seasonings in a large bowl.
4. Place in a single layer in the air fryer basket.
5. Cook for 9-11 minutes shaking the basket frequently so all the sides get crispy and browned.

Frozen Egg Rolls In The Air Fryer

Servings: 5
Cooking Time: 8 Minutes

Ingredients:
- 5 frozen egg rolls

Directions:
1. Preheat your air fryer to 380 degrees.
2. Place the frozen egg rolls in the air fryer not touching and cook them for 8 to 10 minutes.
3. Remove them from the air fryer, let cool slightly, then enjoy!*
4. *reheat at 350 degrees for 3 minutes, preheated

Notes

HOW TO COOK FROZEN SPRING ROLLS IN THE AIR FRYER
Preheat your air fryer to 400 degrees.
Place frozen spring rolls in the air fryer and cook for 7 to 8 minutes until warmed thoroughly. Remove from the air fryer and enjoy!*
*reheat at 350 degrees for 2 to 3 minutes, preheated
HOW TO COOK FROZEN MINI EGG ROLLS IN THE AIR FRYER
Preheat your air fryer to 380 degrees.

101

Place the frozen mini egg rolls in the air fryer and cook for 5 to 7 minutes until warmed thoroughly. Remove them from the air fryer and enjoy!*

*reheat at 350 degrees for about 2 minutes

Air Fryer Spinach, Roasted Red Pepper, And Goat Cheese Omelet

Servings: 1

Ingredients:
- Olive oil cooking spray
- 3 large eggs
- 2 tbsp. whole milk
- Kosher salt
- Freshly ground black pepper
- 3 tbsp. thawed and well-squeezed chopped frozen spinach
- 3 tbsp. finely chopped roasted red peppers
- 1 tbsp. crumbled goat cheese

Directions:
1. Grease a 7" nonstick round cake pan with cooking spray. In a medium bowl, whisk eggs, milk, a large pinch of salt, and a few grinds of black pepper until well combined.
2. Pour egg mixture into prepared pan. Top half of egg mixture with spinach and red peppers. Carefully transfer pan to an air-fryer basket. Cook at 350° until eggs are just set, 6 to 8 minutes.
3. Remove pan from air fryer. Top vegetables with goat cheese. Using a spatula, fold egg over filling. Slide omelet out of pan onto a plate.

Air Fryer Hard Boiled Eggs

Servings: 6

Cooking Time: 15 Minutes

Ingredients:
- 6 large eggs

Directions:
1. Place baking rack in the bowl in the low position. Carefully place eggs on top.
2. Tap the bake button and set temperature to 300°F and fry for 12-14 minutes.
3. Note: 12 minutes for a looser yolk. 14 minutes for a set yolk.
4. Carefully move eggs, with tongs, to a bowl of cold water for 5-10 minutes.
5. Tap eggs on a hard surface and peel.
6. Store in an airtight container in the refrigerator for 3-4 days.

Air Fryer Blueberry Baked Oats

Servings: 4

Cooking Time: 10-30 Minutes

Ingredients:
- 2 free-range eggs
- 400ml/14fl oz milk
- 4 tbsp runny honey or maple syrup
- 200g/7oz porridge oats
- 2 tsp baking powder
- large pinch salt
- 100g/3½oz fresh blueberries or any frozen berries
- plain yoghurt, to serve (optional)

Directions:
1. Beat together the eggs, milk and honey in a large bowl. Add the oats, baking powder and salt to the bowl, stirring until well mixed. If you have time, leave to sit for 5–10 minutes so the oats can soak up the milk. Preheat the air fryer to 175C.
2. Divide the mixture between four small heatproof dishes or 150ml/5fl oz ramekins and then scatter over the blueberries.
3. Air fry for 10–12 minutes until golden and set. Serve warm or chilled, topped with a spoonful of yoghurt, if using.

Recipe Tips

Make the mixture the night before and store covered in the fridge to make breakfast even faster in the morning. Remove from the fridge to allow to come to room temperature before topping with blueberries and cooking.

If you don't have an air fryer you can bake these in an oven preheated to 200C/180C Fan/Gas 6 for 20-25 minutes.

Crispy Spinach Tacos

Servings: 9

Cooking Time: 20 Minutes

Ingredients:

- 9 small spinach tortillas (5-inch diameter)
- 2 cups of (360 g) cooked rice
- 1 (15 oz) can kidney beans or black beans (rinsed and drained)
- 1 small/medium onion diced
- ½ tbsp oil
- 2 garlic cloves minced
- ½ bell pepper chopped
- ¾ cup (100 g) canned mushrooms or use fresh
- ½ tsp onion powder
- ½ tsp ground cumin
- ½ tsp paprika
- ¼ tsp smoked paprika
- ¼ tsp ground ginger (optional)
- ¼ tsp black pepper or more to taste
- sea salt to taste
- 1 tbsp balsamic vinegar
- 1 tbsp soy sauce (gluten-free if needed)
- 4 tbsp plant-based milk
- ⅓ cup (80 g) passata
- 2 tbsp hot sauce (or use less/more to taste)
- 1 batch (200 g) vegan cheese sauce or use 7 oz store-bought vegan cheese

Directions:

1. Cook rice according to package instructions. You will need 2 cups of cooked rice for this recipe.
2. Prepare the spinach tortillas (click for the recipe) or use store-bought flour tortillas or corn tortillas of choice.
3. Meanwhile, heat oil in a pan/skillet over medium heat and add the onion, mushrooms, and bell pepper.
4. Sauté for about 3-5 minutes, then add garlic for a further minute. Stir occasionally.
5. Add all spices, balsamic vinegar, soy sauce, plant-based milk, passata, and hot sauce. Stir and let simmer for about 3 minutes.
6. Add cooked rice and beans, stir and turn off the heat.
7. Taste and adjust seasoning if needed.
8. Preheat oven to 410 degrees Fahrenheit (210 degrees Celsius) and line a baking sheet with parchment paper.
9. Make one batch of the vegan cheese sauce or use store-bought vegan cheese.
10. Add about 2 tbsp of the rice filling on one side of a tortilla and 1 tbsp of the vegan cheese. Fold the other side over the filling and press it slightly down with your fingers (see pictures above in the blog post). Do the same for the remaining tortillas.
11. Transfer all tortillas to the baking sheet. Bake in the oven for about 10-15 minutes, or until crispy. Enjoy hot!
12. Check the blog post for the air-fryer method.

Air Fryer Crispy Breaded Cauliflower Bites

Servings: 2

Cooking Time: 12 Minutes

Ingredients:

- 1/2 pound (227 g) fresh cauliflower, cut into bite sized florets (about 2 cups)
- 1/2 teaspoon (2.5 ml) salt, or to taste
- black pepper, preferably fresh ground
- 1/2 teaspoon (2.5 ml) garlic powder
- Optional Seasonings: Lemon pepper seasoning, paprika, cajun spices, Montreal steak seasoning, etc
- 1 egg, beaten
- 1/2 cup (54 g) bread crumbs (regular or Japanese panko)
- 2 Tablespoons (30 ml) grated parmesan cheese
- Optional Dips: hot sauce, ranch, bbq sauce, etc.
- EQUIPMENT

- Air Fryer
- Perforated Silicone Mats (optional)
- Air Fryer Parchment Paper (optional)
- Oil Sprayer

Directions:
1. Pre-heat air fryer at 360°F/182°C for about 5 minutes.
2. In a bowl, combine the cauliflower florets, salt, pepper, and garlic powder (and any other optional seasoning you prefer). Gently toss to evenly coat the cauliflower. Add beaten egg and stir to coat the cauliflower.
3. In another bowl combine the bread crumbs and parmesan cheese Dip cauliflower florets in the bread crumb mix and gently shake off excess coating.
4. Spray all sides of the breaded cauliflower with oil spray. Dry breading might fly around in air fryer and burn, so make sure to coat any dry spots.
5. Spray air fryer basket/tray with oil (or line with a perforated silicone mat or parchment paper) and place cauliflower in a single layer in the basket/tray.
6. Air Fry at 360°F/182°C for 5-8 minutes. Gently flip and spray any dry spots with oil spray.
7. Air Fry at 360°F/182°C for additional 3-5 minutes or until they are crispy golden brown OR to your preferred texture. Serve warm with your favorite dip.

Air Fryer Breakfast Burritos

Servings: 4
Cooking Time: 6 Minutes

Ingredients:
- 4 eggs
- ¼ cup milk
- ½ teaspoon chili powder
- ¼ teaspoon salt
- ⅛ tablespoon black pepper
- 4 10 inch flour tortillas
- ½ cup shredded cheddar or Colby and Monterey Jack cheese (2 oz.)
- 1 avocado, halved, seeded, peeled, and chopped
- Olive oil or nonstick cooking spray
- Salsa and/or guacamole (optional)

Directions:
1. Preheat air fryer at 400°F. In a 1-qt. casserole or other oven-going dish whisk together eggs, milk, chili powder, salt, and pepper. Place casserole in air-fryer basket. Cook 6 to 8 minutes or until eggs are set, stirring twice. (If air fryer is smaller, divide egg mixture among 10-oz. ramekins and cook in batches.)
2. Divide egg mixture among tortillas. Sprinkle with cheese and top with avocado. Fold in opposite sides and roll up tortillas. Lightly coat burritos with olive oil or cooking spray. Working in batches if needed, arrange burritos in air-fryer basket. Cook 2 to 3 minutes or until toasted. If desired, serve with salsa and/or guacamole.

Tips

After rolling up tortillas, wrap in plastic wrap. Arrange in an airtight container and freeze up to 3 months. To reheat in the air fryer, preheat air fryer to 375°F. Unwrap burritos and arrange in air fryer basket, seam side down. Lightly coat with olive oil or cooking spray. Air fry for 18 minutes or until browned and heated through, turning once halfway through cooking.

Air Fryer Eggplant Parmesan

Servings: 4
Cooking Time: 20 Minutes

Ingredients:
- ½ cup Italian bread crumbs
- ¼ cup freshly grated Parmesan cheese
- 1 teaspoon Italian seasoning
- 1 teaspoon salt
- ½ teaspoon dried basil
- ½ teaspoon garlic powder
- ½ teaspoon onion powder
- ½ teaspoon freshly ground black pepper
- ¼ cup flour
- 2 large eggs, beaten

- 1 medium eggplant, sliced into 1/2-inch rounds
- 1 cup marinara sauce, or more to taste
- 8 slices mozzarella cheese, or as needed

Directions:
1. Combine bread crumbs, Parmesan cheese, Italian seasoning, salt, basil, garlic powder, onion powder, and black pepper in a shallow bowl. Place flour in a separate shallow bowl and beaten eggs in a third shallow bowl.
2. Dip sliced eggplant first in flour, then in beaten eggs, and finally coat with bread crumb mixture. Place coated eggplant on a tray and let rest for 5 minutes.
3. Preheat an air fryer to 370 degrees F (185 degrees C).
4. Place breaded eggplant rounds in the air fryer basket, making sure they are not touching; work in batches if necessary. Cook for 8 to 10 minutes, flip each round, and cook until desired crispiness is achieved, 4 to 6 minutes more.
5. Top each eggplant round with marinara sauce and 1 slice of mozzarella cheese. Place the basket back in the air fryer and cook until cheese has started to melt, 1 to 2 minutes. Repeat with remaining eggplant, if necessary.
6. Serve hot and enjoy!

Air Fryer Mini Egg, Ham, And Cheese Quiche

Servings: 6
Cooking Time: 25 Minutes

Ingredients:
- 4 eggs
- 2 tbsp milk
- ½ cup diced ham or bacon, sausage
- ½ cup cheese shredded
- ½ teaspoon salt & pepper

Directions:
1. Preheat the air fryer to 350°F.
2. Combine all of the ingredients in a bowl and whisk until combined.
3. Place the silicone cups in the air fryer basket and evenly divide the egg mixture filling up the cups 3/4 of the way full.
4. Cover with foil and bake for 20 minutes. Then uncover and cook for 5 more.

Air Fryer Soft Boiled Eggs

Servings: 4
Cooking Time: 6 Minutes

Ingredients:
- 4 large eggs

Directions:
1. Place the eggs in a small ramekin or silicone dish, or in the air fryer basket.
2. Air fry at 300 degrees F for 6-8 minutes. (Six minutes for very runny yolks and whites, 8 minutes for more firm whites, but still slightly runny yolks)
3. When done air frying, place eggs into an ice bath until they are warm to the touch. Gently peel eggs and serve as desired.
4. If using eggs as "dippy eggs," place slightly cooled eggs in egg holders, and gently crack tops with a spoon, and remove the top shells.

Air Fryer Brisket Tacos

Servings: 4
Cooking Time: 12 Minutes

Ingredients:
- 8 small corn tortillas
- 2 cups leftover beef brisket
- ¼ cup red onions diced
- 1 avocado diced
- 1 lime juiced
- 2 tablespoons cilantro chopped
- toppings as desired for serving

Directions:
1. Preheat the air fryer to 400°F.

2. Wrap the tortillas in foil and place in the air fryer for 3-4 minutes or until warmed. Remove from the air fryer and set aside.
3. While the tortillas are warming, combine avocado, red onion, lime, and cilantro in a bowl. Season with salt an set aside.
4. Chop or pull the brisket into pieces and place in the air fryer. Cook 3-5 minutes or until heated through and it begins to crisp.
5. Top each tortilla with ¼ cup of brisket and a spoonful of the salsa mixture.
6. Drizzle with sour cream and a sprinkle of cheese if desired.

Air Fryer Zucchini Pizza Bites

Servings: 4

Cooking Time: 10 Minutes

Ingredients:

- 2 zucchini (medium sized)
- ¾ cup Primal Kitchen's Roasted Garlic Marinara Sauce
- ¾ cup shredded mozzarella cheese
- ½ cup turkey pepperoni
- 1 tbsp olive oil (for spraying)

Directions:

1. Slice the zucchini into slices that are about ¼ inch thick.
2. Lay the zucchini slices flat in the air fryer basket. Do not overcrowd. The zucchini should not overlap. You will need to do this in batches. Spray the slices with olive oil and cook for 3-4 minutes at 400 degrees F.
3. Add the marinara sauce, shredded mozzarella cheese and turkey pepperoni on top of each zucchini slice.
4. Place the basket back into the air fryer and cook for 4-6 minutes at 400 degrees F or until the cheese melts.
5. Repeat as many times as needed depending on the size of your air fryer. As you are making them, let them cool on a wire cooling rack.

Air Fryer Hash Brown Egg Bites

Servings: 7

Ingredients:

- Deselect All
- Nonstick cooking spray, for the mold
- 4 large eggs
- 1/4 cup heavy cream
- Kosher salt
- 2/3 cup shredded Cheddar
- 1/4 cup diced red bell peppers
- 1 scallion, white and green parts sliced
- 1/2 cup shredded frozen hash browns, thawed

Directions:

1. Special equipment: a 7-cavity silicone egg bites mold, 6-quart air fryer
2. Spray the cavities of a 7-cavity silicone egg bites mold with nonstick spray. Whisk together the eggs, heavy cream and 1/2 teaspoon salt in a large glass measuring cup until no white streaks remain.
3. Divide the egg mixture, 1/3 cup of the Cheddar, the bell peppers and scallions among the cavities of the mold. Gently stir the mixture in each cavity with a spoon. Transfer the mold to the basket of a 6-quart air fryer, set it to 300°F and cook for 3 minutes.
4. Meanwhile, combine the hash browns and remaining 1/3 cup Cheddar in a small bowl. Gently top each egg bite with the hash brown-cheese mixture.
5. Set the air fryer to 300°F and cook for 12 minutes more. The top of each bite should be golden brown and the eggs should be set. Remove the mold and let stand for 10 minutes before popping out the egg bites. Serve warm.

Air Fryer Baked Oats

Ingredients:
- 1 cup oats
- 1/2 cup milk of choice
- 1 tablespoon lemon curd flavoured yogurt
- 1 teaspoon baking powder
- 1 banana
- 1 flat teaspoon cinnamon
- 2 teaspoon honey
- 5/6 raspberries
- Dark choc chips

Directions:
1. In a blender blend all your ingredients besides the raspberries and choc chips. Until it's a smooth paste. Pour into ramekins. Top with raspberries and choc chips. Place into your Vortex air fryer to bake on 160 degrees Celsius for 10 minutes then turn to 180 for 2 more minutes.
2. I added a dollop of lemon curd yogurt to the top. This feels like a dessert or baked pudding for breakfast. You can use any variety of toppings and additions, you could use plain yoghurt I just love the combination of raspberries and lemon.

Air Fryer Pasta Tacos

Servings: 4
Cooking Time: 45 Minutes

Ingredients:
- 24 jumbo pasta shells
- 60ml (1/4 cup) extra virgin olive oil
- 1 small red onion, chopped
- 500g beef mince
- 2 tsp ground cumin
- 2 tsp ground coriander
- 1 tsp garlic powder
- 375g jar medium thick 'n' chunky salsa
- 125g can black beans
- 1 1/2 tsp Mexican chilli powder
- 80g (1 cup) grated cheddar
- 2 tomatoes, diced
- 1 avocado, diced
- Fresh coriander sprigs, to serve
- Sour cream, to serve
- Lime cheeks, to serve
- Select all ingredients

Directions:
1. Cook pasta in a large saucepan of boiling, salted water for 10 minutes or until just tender. Using a slotted spoon, transfer pasta to a tray lined with paper towel to drain.
2. Meanwhile, heat half the oil in a large frying pan over medium-high heat. Add onion. Cook, stirring for 5 minutes or until softened. Add mince. Cook, breaking up mince with a wooden spoon, for 5 minutes or until browned. Add cumin, coriander and half the garlic powder. Cook, stirring for 1 minute or until fragrant. Add salsa and beans. Season with salt and pepper. Bring to a simmer. Reduce heat to low. Simmer for 15 minutes.
3. Preheat air fryer on 200C. Combine Mexican chilli powder, remaining garlic powder and oil in a large bowl. Add pasta. Season well with salt and pepper. Toss gently to coat. Spoon mince mixture in pasta shells to fill. Sprinkle with cheese. Place 1/3 of the pasta shells, cheese-side up, in the air fryer basket. Cook for 5-8 minutes or until shells are golden and crispy. Carefully transfer to a large serving plate. Repeat with remaining pasta.
4. Top with combined tomato and avocado. Sprinkle with coriander. Serve with sour cream and lime cheeks.

Air Fryer Avocado Eggs

Servings: 2
Cooking Time: 8 Minutes

Ingredients:

- 2 avocados
- 4 eggs
- salt and pepper to taste
- toppings optional: Salsa, Shredded Cheese, Crumbled Bacon, Hot Sauce

Directions:

1. Line the air fryer basket with parchment paper and set aside.
2. Slice avocado in half, lengthwise, and then carefully remove the pit.
3. Using a spoon, gently remove some of the avocado meat, forming a well where the pit was. Save the removed avocado to top the egg, or to eat separately.
4. Place halves in the air fryer basket, and then carefully crack eggs, breaking direction into each half of the avocado.
5. Air fry at 400 degrees F for 8-12 minutes, depending on how well done you prefer your eggs.
6. Season as desired.

Notes

Variations

Make an avocado toast - If you want to spread the cooked cream avocado on toast and add a bit of Bagel seasoning, you can create an avocado mixture on bread in no time at all. Simple ingredients can easily make all sorts of an easy breakfast.

Add feta cheese - Putting feta cheese on top of the fried egg sounds awesome. This is a simple way that you can make air fryer-baked eggs with an avocado half taste different easily.

Make it spicy - Add some sweet chili sauce to the top of avocado eggs for a spicy hot flavor combination. You can skip the sweet and add red pepper flakes as well.

Pair with other breakfast foods - Make it a large meal by adding some hash browns, turkey bacon, or even fresh fruit.

Air Fryer Frozen Hash Brown Patties

Servings: 4
Cooking Time: 15 Minutes

Ingredients:

- 4 Frozen Hash Brown Patties
- salt , optional to taste
- black pepper , optional to taste
- EQUIPMENT
- Air Fryer

Directions:

1. Place the frozen hash brown patties in the air fryer basket and spread in an even layer (make sure they aren't overlapping). No oil spray is needed.
2. Air Fry at 380°F/193°C for 10 minutes. Flip the hashbrown patties over.
3. Continue to Air Fry at 380°F/193°C for an additional 2-5 minutes or until crisped to your liking. Season with salt & pepper, if desired.

Notes

Air Frying Tips and Notes:

No Oil Necessary. Cook Frozen - Do not thaw first.

Turn as needed. Cook in a single layer in the air fryer basket.

Recipe timing is based on a non-preheated air fryer. If cooking in multiple batches back to back, the following batches may cook a little quicker.

Recipes were tested in 3.7 to 6 qt. air fryers. If using a larger air fryer, the hash browns might cook quicker so adjust cooking time.

Remember to set a timer to flip as directed in recipe.

Printed in Great Britain
by Amazon